No Labels Here

of related interest

The Family Experience of PDA
An Illustrated Guide to Pathological Demand Avoidance
Eliza Fricker
Foreword by Ruth Fidler
ISBN 978 1 78775 677 9
eISBN 978 1 78775 678 6

Can't Not Won't
A Story About A Child Who Couldn't Go To School
Eliza Fricker
ISBN 978 1 83997 520 2
eISBN 978 1 83997 521 9

Parenting Rewired
How to Raise a Happy Autistic Child in a Very Neurotypical World
Danielle Punter and Charlotte Chaney
ISBN 978 1 83997 072 6
eISBN 978 1 83997 073 3

A Different Way to Learn
Neurodiversity and Self-Directed Education
Naomi Fisher
ISBN 978 1 83997 363 5
eISBN 978 1 83997 364 2

NO LABELS HERE

A Day-to-Day Guide for Parenting Children with Neurodiverse Needs

Eve Marie Bent

Jessica Kingsley Publishers

London and Philadelphia

First published in Great Britain in 2024 by Jessica Kingsley Publishers
An imprint of John Murray Press

1

Front cover image source: Shutterstock®.

A CIP catalogue record for this title is available from the
British Library and the Library of Congress

ISBN 978 1 83997 376 5
eISBN 978 1 83997 377 2

Printed and bound in Great Britain by TJ Books Ltd

Jessica Kingsley Publishers' policy is to use papers that are natural,
renewable and recyclable products and made from wood grown in
sustainable forests. The logging and manufacturing processes are expected
to conform to the environmental regulations of the country of origin.

Jessica Kingsley Publishers
Carmelite House
50 Victoria Embankment
London EC4Y 0DZ

www.jkp.com

John Murray Press
Part of Hodder & Stoughton Ltd
An Hachette Company

MIX
Paper from
responsible sources
FSC® C013056

Contents

This is for you Dad – I did it!

To my wonderful husband and children, thank you for your time and patience in supporting me. Thank you for the laughter and tears that helped to write this book. You are all my world, and I wouldn't have our hectic, loud, topsy-turvy home any other way.

And to the amazing women, friends and family that have got me through motherhood so far – thank you! I found my people; my support, strength and pillars – you are what every mother needs.

Introduction

Hello!

My name is Eve, and I am a mother, a wife, an academic and, at times, a hot mess. You would find it amazing how long it took me to write that first sentence. To gather everything you are in all parts of your life into one sentence is difficult, and to me, it still doesn't feel right – I am more than the sum of my roles. Nevertheless, for the majority of my adult life, I have been a mother. I had my first child (Molly) when I was 19 years old, the same year I married my husband. From then, my life – our lives – revolved around being parents. Although we have both worked our entire adult lives, we have always put family first – we often say the mantra 'work to live; don't live to work'. That's not to say we don't both enjoy our jobs and careers, because we really do, but we have always known that family comes first. Family is there in the good times to celebrate your victories, and there in the bad times to give you that big hug you need. Family is everything to us.

That might help you understand why, after having Molly, we continued to have Charlotte, Samuel and Teddy. Now, ask any parent of more than three children, and sometimes more than two children, and they will tell you that those unsolicited comments will come flying at you – as if the number of children you have is the business of anyone else in the world. Yes, we have had it all – 'Don't you have a TV?' 'Are you trying for a football team?' 'You're like the Von Trapp family' – and we are now impervious to it, although I cannot say it didn't used to hurt. We love children – their intriguing minds, their hilarious sense of humour, their wonderful and weird knowledge of random things and how they want to tell you all about them at the most random and inconvenient times. To us, welcoming more children was an absolute blessing, and we adore having our house full, busy and noisy (I would add messy – but I don't particularly enjoy that part!). When one or two of the children go out to sleepovers with friends or with grandparents, the house just feels so empty and quiet, even with two or three children still at home.

That is the family side of my life – my wonderful crazy family. I will go on to introduce you to them all later, and you will get to know them very well through the rest of the book.

Bringing up my family is my most important job, but as I mentioned earlier, I have always been a working mum. I took a somewhat unconventional route to where I am now, but I am glad of every step of it – as corny as that sounds! As was common when I was younger, I started a part-time weekend job when I was 13 (something that now horrifies my Gen-Z teenagers). Since then, I have tried my hand at being a waitress, working a fast-food drive-through window, fitting men's wedding suits, being a telesales ticket booker and being a bookmaker. When I left college after completing my A-levels, I knew I wanted to do something to make a difference in children's lives, but I wasn't sure what that was. I went to Manchester University to study social work with children. Looking back, I was naive about the stresses of university, and I didn't get the support I needed at the time. By the end of the first semester, I fell into a spiral of depression, struggling with poor housing, overwhelmed with academic commitments and finding no support – so I dropped out. At this point in my life, I thought academia wasn't for me. I am dyslexic, I couldn't handle university and I thought I would never complete my degree. I still wanted to help children, though, in whatever way I could, so I began working as a nursery assistant in the hope of working my way up the ladder with on-the-job training.

That's exactly what I did. I started as a nursery assistant, worked up to nursery nurse and room leader, and eventually opened and managed a nursery for a local entrepreneur. In my time in nurseries, I worked with hundreds of young children and their families, all with varying abilities and needs. I saw children who were loved and cared for, and, unfortunately, children who weren't. I acted as a safeguarding lead, protecting the most vulnerable among us, and I acted as a special educational needs coordinator (SENCo), advocating for children who couldn't advocate for themselves. The length and breadth of knowledge and experience I gained in these roles is immense and invaluable. While in my final nursery position, as nursery manager, I completed my degree in young children's learning and development, which was something I never thought I would be able to do after my first experiences of university.

Unfortunately, that's when things took a downward turn. Samuel had just been born and had many medical needs as a baby, so I became a full-time carer and mum to him for several years. At the time, that was the best thing for him and for our family, and, looking back, it changed my whole journey for the better.

When Samuel was two years old, my mind couldn't stay still and I longed to learn more, so I began a second degree in psychology, at first part-time and then moving to full-time after a year. It was through this degree that I took on roles in the developmental psychology lab at the university. I was awarded grants to conduct my own research, and I fell in love with developmental psychology and doing all I could to make a difference to all children, not just the ones in my care. As I will go on to explain below, this came at a time when Samuel was going through several hard years, pre-diagnosis, and we had so much stress in our lives. However, having the knowledge I gained from my experience and my studies, I felt more equipped than ever to understand what my son needed from me and how we as parents could help him. After completing my psychology degree and taking a year's break to have Teddy, I stepped back into academia, both with my first graduate-level academic role as a project officer for an autism project and as a PhD student researching autism and digital media. My path wasn't conventional by any means, and it certainly had its challenges, but every part of it brought me the knowledge and experience that I hold today, and that is something I will always be grateful for.

As I mentioned earlier, the biggest part of my life is my family. My wonderful, unique, big family. I met my husband, Chris, when we were at college; I was a mere 16 years old and he was 17 – young love. We faced comments and criticisms for staying together so young, but here we are 19 years later and still going strong. We were married and had Molly young, but that worked for us, and we wouldn't go back and change it (mainly because we now have a teenager who is nearly at babysitting age for the younger ones!). Chris joined the police in 2008 and has been there ever since, working hard day and night to provide for his family. He's really been our rock year after year.

Less than two years after we had Molly, we had Charlotte. The small age gap was hard, but we were glad to get all the nappies done with in one go – or so we thought. When Molly was five and Charlotte was three, we welcomed Samuel into our lives. Our beautiful little boy after two girls. As I mentioned earlier, Samuel wasn't a well baby. Arriving five weeks early and with a huge collection of allergies and medical issues, much of his early life was spent between hospital and doctor's appointments. Eventually, though, we got everything under control and fell into our own little rhythm of life. We knew what to avoid, where we could take him that was safe, and we got to grips with epi-pens and everything that came with severe allergies.

Then, as Samuel developed, we noticed little differences in him that we didn't see in the girls. He was quieter, he didn't want to play with us or anyone, he didn't babble away while he played with his toys, and his play was very structured. Does anyone else recognise lines of cars in their home? Eventually, more and more traits became obvious to us. With my experience of working with special educational needs (SEN) children in childcare, I could spot the small idiosyncrasies and mannerisms, subtle as they were. Samuel began having a very difficult relationship with sensory items; clothes became difficult for him to wear (anyone else's child walk around naked in the house?), and food just became a nightmare for us as his diet was reduced to just a hand-ful of foods. We asked for Samuel to be referred for an autism assessment when he was five years old, and he finally reached that diagnosis when he was eight and a half – a full three and a half years after we began begging for support. Those three and a half years were the hardest of our lives. We were drowning and we knew the lifeboat was coming...but it was on a waiting list somewhere on someone's desk. We had to learn how to cope with meltdowns, school refusal, not eating, not dressing, eloping, violence and so much more, all on our own. We had to try to find our own community while always feeling not part of the community because we didn't yet have that magic diagnosis that unlocks all the doors to support. Then, in 2019, we were blessed with our second son, Teddy. A wonderful bundle of joy, and with no other children in nappies or even remotely small (Samuel was seven by the time Teddy was born), we were thrown back into the world of newborns. Thankfully, we had never regained sleep after Samuel (maybe not so thankfully!) and we were able to fit the newborn Teddy into our lives almost too easily. Teddy was doing amazingly well. The Covid-19 pandemic meant that we had so much more time at home to care for him rather than being out at work, and we also used this time to bond as a family and make the most of what we could in pandemic times. But it was later, after the UK lockdown, when Teddy was around 13 months old, that we began to notice changes in his behaviour, a regression in language, a lack of understanding...and so the road less travelled is where we started again. Referrals, waiting lists, appointments and more – a road we are still travelling now. Thankfully, the second time round, the professionals seem to value our knowledge and opinion more, which shouldn't be the case. We have been able to get a diagnosis of autism for Teddy much more quickly than for Samuel, but the waiting and the limbo were still a huge part of our lives for a long time. As our children have got older and developed into wonderful young adults, our challenges have increased. At one point, I thought the toddler years were difficult (oh, how I wish we still had that level of difficulty!), but once your children become teenagers, so much can change – particularly in girls. When our eldest reached 14, she was struggling with many things, and after some assessments, we were told that she was also neurodiverse – she has attention deficit hyperactive disorder (ADHD). And like a wheel that never stops spinning, our youngest daughter reached 14 this year and, lo and behold, her school has approached us about her needing assessments for neurodiversities.

And so we sit here with you, watching and waiting, calling the professionals endlessly and begging for support. We are your community now.

Why I wanted to write this book

When I began thinking about this book, about what it would be and who it would be for, it wasn't hard at all for me to narrow down who I wanted to support. For years, I have stalked online forums and groups looking for support. Feeling as if we had all these issues and nowhere to turn, no one to help us. Out there in those digital forums, I found a community; I found people who are living the same life and experiences as we are. I found parents who were also awake at 3 a.m. (and not with a newborn!); parents whose children lashed out at them, and they didn't know what to do; parents who, like us, were exhausted, beaten down and broken. I found my people. And what I have learned in the years following is that there are so many of us. Parents who don't know if they are part of the autism community because they don't have that elusive diagnosis, but parents nonetheless who are dealing with exactly the same behaviours and challenges they will face when they do finally get the diagnosis for their child. This pre-diagnosis community sits in limbo-land for years before they are offered any kind of formal support from health and community services. We have been there: it took us three and a half years to get Samuel's final diagnosis because he is an amazing, intelligent, articulate young man. He has the ability to mask, to know when he has to hold it all in, but he also has so many social and communication struggles that filter into every part of his life that some support pre-diagnosis would have made all the difference, both to him and to us as parents.

At the time of writing, the current UK waiting time from referral to diagnosis is around three years, and in the USA this stands at around three and a half years, mostly because there are such large numbers of children being sent through the diagnosis process. Gone are the days when children were labelled as 'naughty' or 'rude'; both parents and practitioners are rightly recognising the need for adequate formal assessment of children in order to support them more robustly as they grow older. Although this is a positive step in the understanding of children, it also creates significant backlogs in waiting times, with not enough practitioners, money or resources to support the systems children are being referred to. The doctors and practitioners themselves are doing their best, and from personal experience, everyone we have met has been wonderful, thorough and giving their all. But they are working in systems not set up to support this amount of pressure, and unfortunately the pressure is resting on the children and parents waiting for diagnosis.

This book aims to bridge the gap between those first concerns around your child until the time you get your diagnosis and beyond. Unlike many books out there, my aim isn't to support you with 'autism' or 'ADHD' per se. My aim is to support you as parents with the practical day-to-day challenges that you may be having with your child – whatever their final diagnosis is. This book aims to be a go-to guide to help and support you in different aspects of your life. We will cover hints and tips for supporting your child as well as real, lived experience, either my own or that of people who have shared with me. I hope this book can be a guide for you to pop in and out of as you need to, to use in a fluid way, changing with your needs and the needs of your child or children. But most of all, I hope this book provides you as parents with a little reassurance that what you are going through is common, that your fears and worries are similar to those of parents who have walked this path before you, and that there are people out there who are your people, who you can call your community. I want my readers to understand that you belong and that you have every right to use the 'neurodiversity' help pages and forums. You have every right to ask for the lanyards if they will support your child, to ask for adjustments to your child's education or support when out and about. You have a right to be in this space – because this is your experience as much as it is the experience of someone with a diagnosis. Be there for your child's needs rather than their label.

A note about language

As we continue into the heart of the book, I just want to share with you how I am going to use language, particularly regarding autism. Although the book will cover all neurodiversities and neurodiverse challenges, the language surrounding autism is itself diverse and often a point of contention. The difficulty around language often comes from misunderstanding or mis-representation, so I always believe it is best to be open and clear right from the start. I have mostly found that no matter what language people use, they are usually aiming for the same out-come: respect, understanding, awareness and acceptance for the autism community. When words and actions come from a good place like this, to me, the language becomes much less important. I have had messages asking for advice before now, often with a precursory note to excuse the writer if they are not using the correct terminology – this isn't something I would ever want to promote. I hope the conversation around language can continue with love and good intentions, improving the knowledge and awareness of everybody as a means to better support autistic individuals.

That being said, there are words or phrases I will use in the book, and I would like to clarify why I will be using them. The first of these is 'autistic'. There was a time not too long ago when person-centred language was preferred (such as 'a person with autism') and, in many parts of the autism community, it still is. Collectively, however, the community has moved on in our conversation around autism, and now it is recognised that autism is an integral part of a person and their character and shouldn't be seen as separate. For this reason, you will see me talking about an autistic child or adult or even my autistic son. If this is not how you would describe yourself or your child, that's perfectly okay. The discussion around language is an important one, and we all take different views on things. Just know that for the purposes of this book, this is the language that I will use.

You will have noticed me referring to the 'autism community'. By using this phrase, I am referring to autistic individuals, adults and children, parents and carers. As with many things surrounding autism, wording and labels are hotly debated. Some autistic adults don't believe that those who are not diagnosed with autism should be included in the 'autism community'. However, from my experience, both personal and professional, there is no part of autism that doesn't affect those around the autistic individual, and for that reason, when I refer to the autism community throughout the book, you should take this to mean all those who are autistic or are affected personally by autism in their lives. And in the same way as 'autism community', you may also see references to 'autism family', 'autism parent' or 'autism mum'. These labels do not attempt to take away from the daily struggles of those who have autism; they simply serve as a descriptive tool to allow you, the reader, to understand the relationship I am describing with the autistic person. It is important to understand from the point of view of a carer of an autistic individual, particularly one of young age or with predominantly challenging needs, that part of their identity does become the caring role for the individual, and for so many people in that role, there isn't a community out there that understands other than the autistic community.

Similarly, I refer to 'neurodiversities' and 'neurodiverse individuals' or similar. By this, I mean anyone who has signs and symptoms of neurodiverse conditions, such as autism, ADHD, dyslexia, dyscalculia, foetal alcohol syndrome, etc. The word 'neurodiverse' simply means that the brain (neuro) is not developed in a typical way (unlike a neurotypical brain). This isn't a bad thing; it just means that the brain has developed in a different way. There are many theories for why this is, but we don't always know. Having a neurodiverse brain can be an amazing benefit, as well as sometimes having its challenges. Personally, I have found having a neurodiverse brain has made me super organised, because my brain feels so messy all the time. As our Grandy used to tell us, 'A place for everything, and everything in its place.'

Chapter 1

Good Morning!

Good morning! Kind of a redundant phrase when you have been up all night with a child who does not sleep. I get that, I really get that! Nonetheless, morning is here, the sun has risen (or not in the depths of winter) and it's time to get those beautiful cherubs out of bed and off to start their day – wherever that may be. Mornings with kids are hectic as hell! Someone can't find a shoe, another doesn't want to brush their teeth, and you're making four different kinds of breakfast and desperately trying to get a coffee into your system before you all rush out of the door. But when you add a neurodiverse child (or two or three) into the mix, mornings become a lot more complicated. In this chapter, I aim to go through the morning from eyes open to out of the door and take a practical approach to getting things done. I will provide you with some tips and tricks that I have picked up over the years and share some stories of when things have gone well...and when things have gone wrong. There are no promises that these tips and tricks will solve all or any of your problems, but I will do my best to support you in any way I can with getting out of the door with just a little bit of sanity intact.

First, it is important to mention that I will be discussing the morning as if it is a school or nursery morning – basically, a weekday morning. However, the principles for weekdays are just as applicable to any day of the week when you need to get out of the door in a timely manner.

The night before

It may seem strange to be discussing the night before in a chapter about the morning, but one of the things I have found over the years is that preparation is absolutely everything when it comes to kids. Our morning routine starts the night before we go anywhere, and I think it's so routine to us now that we don't even realise we are doing it. For the children at primary and high school, making sure they have clean uniform laid out is the first thing we do. Not only making sure that it is ready but physically placing it out at the ends of the beds so it is all in easy reach in the morning. This includes socks, underwear, ties, shoes, trousers, skirts, shirts...basically, anything that touches their bodies.

Now, my two eldest children are 12 and 14, so you would think they could make sure they have their uniform out, and I'm sure they could too...about 80 per cent of the time. But what I don't want is for the other 20 per cent of the time, when they can't find a sock or a tie or a shoe, to hit me at 8 a.m. the next morning when the toddler is screaming and my eldest son is anxious about school. So we get it all out the night before – just in case. The girls do get their own things out, but it gives me time to check that they haven't forgotten anything before we reach the morning. My eldest son doesn't have the skills of follow-through to get his own uniform ready yet, something common in autistic children, so we do that together. He is, however, religious about where his shoes are! So I suppose that's one thing I never have to worry about. And, of course, I get the toddler's clothes out for him because I am the only person in the house who can make sure his outfit matches!

When I was in hospital having our eldest son, the girls were three and four years old. They were still in private nursery, where I actually also worked at the time, and my husband was in sole charge of their care while I lay in hospital for a week due to complications. All was fine until I got a message from a colleague asking if I had seen what the girls were wearing that day. I replied saying I had not and their daddy had brought them into nursery. I was very dutifully informed it was photo day at nursery! Daddy had, of course, tried his best and they were clean and warm, but not necessarily matching. As I recall, one of them was wearing a green pullover with a blue skirt, and the other was in dungarees and a very un-matched T-shirt. We did, in fact, get the photos from photo day anyway because the girls are just too cute and can basically rock any outfit, but yes, we leave Mummy to do the children's clothes in this house!

Once the clothes are done, we continue to prepare the rest of the things we will need. The older children get their bags ready for school. My eldest daughter struggles to remember what she may need, and for years we just thought she lacked follow-through or foresight. However, since getting her ADHD diagnosis, we now realise it's a key element of her neurodiversity. It's not that she cannot be bothered to think of what she might need and plan ahead; rather, her brain simply will not let her use those skills effectively. Therefore we make sure we go through what they may need with both the older girls. Pencil, ruler and pen are essentials for their school, and they get logged with negative points if they don't have these. So I keep a stack of spares on my workspace ready to replace (almost daily) when they are lost. Because it turns out that modern teenagers are way too cool to use pencil cases! Apparently, carrying everything around in your blazer pocket and just waiting for the day your pen explodes all over your shirt is way cooler. Not to sound old, but when I attended high school, our pencil cases were a key feature in hiding our mobile phones from our teachers. This was a time when mobile phones were very new (I'm talking Nokia 3210 and Snake!) and you weren't allowed them in school. Now they use their phones for classroom quizzes and all sorts of things. I do understand how old I sound right now, so I shall stop digressing.

Lunches are next. Fortunately for us, the older two buy school meals and the youngest is provided food in childcare, but our eldest son has a very limited diet both due to anaphylactic allergies and because he has avoidant and restrictive food intake disorder (ARFID), something that is closely linked to autism. So he always takes a packed lunch, and it is always the same things – but I shall discuss that more in Chapter 4.

Finally, the last part of the prep for the night before is making sure everyone knows the plan for the morning. Children with neurodiversities often struggle with any changes in routine or things happening unexpectedly. Therefore, every night before the children go to bed, we discuss what will be happening the next day – even if it is a regular weekday and the same routine as normal. I find that by doing this they can go to bed settled at the thought of what is coming in the morning and can mentally prepare themselves for the day in the same way we do as adults. I don't know about you, but I often lie in bed at night going through all the things I need to do the next day and all the tasks I need to accomplish for the day; our children need to have the chance to do that too. It is easy to worry that discussing the next day will get your child worked up or anxious about the day ahead, particularly if they don't like what's going to happen (perhaps they are having difficulties at school), and, honestly, I can't promise you that it won't. However, in my experience both personally and professionally, it is always better to discuss these things upfront, openly and honestly, and deal with any issues as they come up. It is unfair to spring something on a neurodiverse child and not give them the respect of allowing them processing time to think about what is going to happen. Don't get me wrong, I know how much easier it would be to just not mention anything, have a calm bedtime and then tell them in the morning – I've often been very tempted myself. But children need to process, and neurodiverse children need this more than most. Even if the reaction isn't what you had hoped for, know that you are doing the right thing allowing them to feel their feelings, and take the time to discuss any worries with them. Sometimes this can be a delicate balance. We find the first day of the new school year in September is a huge challenge, and so the balance between discussing going back to school and not overwhelming the children is a really hard line to walk, but it must be done. I will discuss this more in Chapter 3.

Wake up early

I know, I know: you want those extra ten minutes in bed; you've had barely any sleep as it is and you're exhausted. I get you – honestly, you don't know how much I agree. However, getting up just ten minutes before the children can make such a huge difference – or so I have been told. Imagine waking up on your own terms, going to the bathroom in peace (I think I have forgotten what that's like at this point), making a cup of coffee and even having the time to drink it! Or simply just lying there and preparing yourself mentally for the day. As much as we want the best for our children, it's also important to remember to take some time for ourselves, and for a lot of parents with children with neurodiversities, this time before they even wake could be the only minute in the day we get alone. So cherish it if you can, because as soon as they wake, chaos is likely to ensue!

Now I'm afraid to say that this is one piece of advice that I have acquired from others, and I do not always practise what I preach. I say this to be completely honest with you; I am by no means perfect and I really love my sleep, particularly when it has been stolen from me on so many occasions by small humans who want to be awake all night. But those wise parents who have provided me with this advice appear to be a lot more put together and ready for the day, so they can't be doing too much wrong. If, like me, you really value your sleep, why not do what I do and try to do it every few days or even once a week? Just to give yourself that space and a head start to the day.

Which leads nicely into the next suggestion...

Get up in plenty of time

Children need time to wake up, shake off the grump and come round for the day. Some children are really good at this and can do it really quickly – my oldest daughter is a prime example. However, some children need coaxing out of bed, and this really isn't their fault. Biologically, children need a lot more sleep than adults; their brains are developing so much during their early years, and all those neurons firing around require lots and lots of sleep. Not only that but their bodies are growing and getting stronger every day – a lot of this growth is happening when they are asleep, and even when it's not, it certainly makes them more tired than we adults feel. I say this so that when you are standing at the end of your child's bed, asking them to wake up for the tenth time that morning, you might just take a breath and wait before starting the shouting (easier said than done). They really aren't being obstructive and uncooperative – it's biological. So if your child does have a habit of not being able to get out of bed the first, second or tenth time you call them, be aware of this and plan it into your morning routine. Start the process half an hour before you actually need them to get up – and hope that is enough time. For a neurodiverse child, moving from one activity to the next can be difficult, even if this is something they do every day. Therefore, planning enough time in the morning to give them time to adjust to the different stages of the morning will only make your morning go more smoothly.

Getting dressed

Getting children dressed in the morning in most households is certainly no easy feat, particularly if they are young. But children always seem to have a knack of knowing when you're in a rush and taking extra-long to get dressed on those days! Nonetheless, they still have to leave the house and so they still need to get dressed. Or do they?

When I was working in a nursery (daycare) years ago, we had one child who did not like clothes. Or certainly did not like clothes at 8 o'clock in the morning when he needed to be dropped off at nursery. After weeks of Mum and Dad fighting with him every single morning, spending countless hours arguing and making their mornings fraught, they eventually came to the realisation that it wasn't going to kill them or their son to wear his pyjamas in public. If anything, it was the best thing for them all. So the young boy came in every day in his pyjamas, and by the time of the first nappy change, he was ready to change into his day clothes with us and pack away the pyjamas. But it meant that his morning was calmer, Mum and Dad's morning was calmer and, most importantly, they all got to enjoy their mornings together again before Mum and Dad had to leave for work.

Now, don't get me wrong: I am not suggesting you send your child to school still dressed in their pyjamas (although I have considered it sometimes). But I am aware of just how difficult it is to get a child out of the door when they won't get dressed.

A significant part of many different neurodiversities is sensory dysregulation. We have many senses. You will know most of them, such as sight (visual), sound (auditory), touch (tactile), smell (olfactory) and taste (gustatory), but we have two other senses that not everyone is aware of – proprioception (sense of position of the body) and vestibular (sense of balance and movement). These senses work together to help us make sense of the world around us. However, in some children (and adults, but here we are talking specifically about children), these senses are not as regulated by the body as they should be. This can lead to a child feeling overwhelmed and out of control (we will continue to discuss this in Chapter 2). This is often what can happen when you are trying to get your child dressed for the day.

Imagine you are your child: you feel every touch of clothes against your skin 100 per cent more than you do now. Now let's imagine you are getting dressed for school...

You put your underwear on and it's close-fitting – you can feel the elastic, the label itches and the seams are rubbing against your hips. You then place your trousers or skirt on top of that and it pushes into your legs even more. The material feels scratchy and weird against your legs...you much preferred your soft pyjamas. Now it's time for your shirt – it has a collar, and you don't like collars because you can feel them all up the back of your neck. Your jumper comes on next – it's tight and you feel as if you are being squeezed; Mummy says it's fine but it feels like you can't move. It's pushing the label on your collar now and it's rubbing against your neck. Now socks – they have a seam against your toes and it's all you can feel...as well as the label on your shirt, and the tight waistband, and the label on your underwear which is still itching. Now shoes – tight shoes. They are stiff and hard and make your feet feel twice as heavy. Plus, everything else is still rubbing and itching...so you decide to strip it all off. But now you're in trouble.

If every sense is feeling more than it should be, when we ask our children to get dressed, we are not just asking for a simple task to be completed. I've asked you to imagine this scenario to help you understand what a herculean task our children are undertaking, and how proud of them you should be every single day they get dressed or even try to get dressed.

Breakfast

So we have woken up, we have finally managed to get washed and dressed, we're all exhausted and the day has not even begun. It is now time to get some food in these children before they leave for the day. As a parent, I have always had one hard and fast rule, no matter which of my children I am dealing with: you do not go out of the house without food in your stomach. Each parent or carer may have their own ideas about this, but for me this is non-negotiable. I would rather my children miss the first ten minutes of school than sit there for four hours until lunch, hungry and unable to concentrate. Breakfast sets you up for the day; it gets your stomach moving and it wakes your body up. There have been numerous studies on the benefits of breakfast and all of them will tell you the importance of eating breakfast every day. Your brain is like an engine in a car – to get the car to run, you have to add fuel. In the same way, you have to add fuel to your body to be able to get your brain to work. The average adult uses 20 per cent of their total calorie intake to power their brain, but children's brains are still developing; they are still learning and absorbing information, making new connections. It's been estimated that up to 50 per cent of a child's calorie intake may be needed to support their brain function. So it's our job as parents to make sure they are getting the best possible start to the day.[1]

As a parent with a child with ARFID, I am no stranger to what a task this may become. Use the tools you know to get what you can into your child. For my older children, this unfortunately (for me) means bribery. They agree to have breakfast if I agree it can be school sausage muffins and give them money for them. This is not ideal as they are leaving the house without food, but I know they can get their food before school starts and have fuel for the day (they also know I can check they have got it through the school app). For the younger children, it's a little more difficult. One will basically only eat a diet of fruit, and so he gets fruit. The other will currently only eat bread, and so he gets toast, cut in a certain way, with only the spread he likes and on a particular plate. As I said, you've got to do what you've got to do sometimes. The point I am trying to make is that the benefits of having some food in your stomach far outweigh the need for you to fight over it being bran flakes with oat milk. When you are a parent of a neurodiverse child, you have to consider the bigger picture. Can my child tolerate the food I want them to have? Does it cause a flare-up of their sensory issues? Does trying something new trigger their anxiety? Is having their toast cut in a different way going to start a two-hour meltdown that will leave us both fraught? These are important questions, and no food is worth that two-hour meltdown, I promise you. Of course, as a responsible parent, you know it is important to try to get your children to eat a healthy diet – I don't think I know a parent who doesn't know that. But there is a balance that applies when you have a neurodiverse child – a balance between their physical health benefiting from a single meal and their mental health suffering from a prolonged battle over a bowl of Shreddies.

Visual timetables

One way to add to the smooth transition between the stages of the morning is to provide your child with a visual timetable of what is expected of them during that routine. Children process visual information at a much faster speed than they process language, so providing a visual support can help them more than telling them the same thing again and again.

A visual timetable also serves a second function: it provides a child, no matter what age, with autonomy. Neurodiverse children, including those with autism spectrum disorder, ADHD, dyslexia and others, often have issues with their motor planning skills. These skills require us to understand what task needs to be completed, plan how we are going to complete the task and then perform the action of completing the task. If your child has difficulties doing simple tasks, following through on instructions or forgetting what they were meant to be doing halfway through, it is likely they have motor planning difficulties. Therefore, giving them their own pictures of what is expected of them in the morning routine (or any routine) gives your child the opportunity to see for themselves what is next and do it each time – without having to remember a long list of instructions one after another.

Visual timetables are also a great way for your child to learn to recognise that changes are coming up. On a morning timetable, you might put pictures of waking up, brushing teeth, getting dressed, eating breakfast and putting coats on. As adults, we understand these are all part of one routine – the morning routine – but for a child who struggles with change, these five activities represent five different activities in five different places requiring five different sets of skills – imagine how overwhelming that could be. As adults, we are aware of what is coming up next, but our children may not remember from yesterday what change is about to happen. Therefore, the visual timetable gives them time to mentally prepare for the next step of their morning routine without it being sprung on them.

A lot of people I see and speak to worry that to be able to provide their children with the things they need, such as visual timetables, they will have to spend a lot of money on cards and pictures being made. You are more than welcome to go and buy pictures that represent your morning, and there are lots of wonderful companies that can make these for you. But let's keep this simple. All your child needs is a basic representation of what their morning may consist of. This may be a piece of A4 paper with little cartoon squares on it – I promise your child will not judge your drawing skills. You may choose to make your own little cards using clipart and print them out, or even take photos of the things you will be doing and have those laid out. It really does not have to cost the earth or be fancy, as long as it is functional for your child.

Cues

I recognise that picture cards and symbols aren't going to work for every family, particularly if the child you're looking for advice for is a teenager.

Before our eldest daughter was diagnosed with ADHD, we used to think she was the most forgetful child in the world. She could be told to get her shoes on and, ten seconds later, forget what she was meant to be doing. During her first year at senior school, she was just hysterically awful at remembering things (I laugh now...I do not think I was laughing back then!). Every day, I would get a phone call from school: 'She has forgotten her pencil and pen', 'She has forgotten her inhaler', 'She has forgotten her ID card.' Every day, I would have to take time out of work to go running back home, get the missing item and drop it off at the school. An errand that caused my patience to run very thin very quickly.

Forgetfulness happens to us all, but when your child is neurodiverse, it can happen an awful lot more. It's frustrating for the person running around, bringing everything they need, but, honestly, they really cannot help it and it's important to remember that. The particular neurodiversity your child has will determine how their brain functions. They may struggle with attention, working memory, problem solving, motor planning or more. They could even be trying to navigate life struggling in more than one of these areas, which is really common among neurodiverse children.

So, how do we help them get out of the house with everything they need? One way you could do this is by using cues or Post-its. This is similar to the idea of a visual timetable. Placing small but noticeable notes around the house can trigger a memory that they need to do something. Everyone needs the bathroom when they wake up, but they might need a note reminding them to shower and clean their teeth. I promise they are not trying to be smelly teenagers – they honestly do not even consider it sometimes until it is mentioned. Wherever they go to collect their bag, keep a list on the wall next to it of things they need – books, pencil case, homework. My favourite is a big note on the back of the door with the essentials on it. Ours currently reads: 'Keys?', 'Inhaler?', 'ID pass?' and 'Phone?' It may seem like going back to basics, but it can make all the difference to a young person who is trying their best to get out of the door but keeps forgetting what it was that they needed. I was recently told that because my son is nearly ten, he should be getting his own things ready for school the night before. To some extent, I agree with this: it is important for our children to learn life skills that will help them prepare themselves and take care of themselves in the future. However, it is also extremely important to understand the very real day-to-day challenges that our children face, including packing their own bags and getting off to school. Therefore, used in conjunction with the other tips mentioned, these Post-its may just get your child to school on time with everything they need.

Positivity

The final piece of advice I can provide for the morning routine is to keep the positivity. It sounds simple, but it is really not. I do understand how hard you're trying and how challenging it can be – I have been there...and I am often back there. I see you. You are so tired, you have got up early to have your cup of tea, you have been up late prepping the night before, and you have navigated several near misses throughout the morning that could have easily led to meltdowns. However, keeping that positivity among it all is going to help teach your child a huge amount of resilience. They will learn that even when things are difficult, when shoes don't feel right and when labels are itchy, they can continue and they can still be okay. Having a positive mental attitude or 'growth mindset' has scientifically been proven to improve outcomes.[2] Believing you can do something will actually help you do something – a skill that all our children will find invaluable throughout life. I often refer to it as keeping your calm in a storm. For our children, their whole worlds can often feel too big, too loud, too chaotic. It can feel like everything is too much, and this is where a child may revert to their fight, flight or freeze mode. To be the calm in the storm means to be the one they look to – not flustered, not upset, not shouting, just calm. You see that things are going wrong, and instead of panicking, you make a plan and you change direction. Keeping that level head throughout your morning will do more good than you can know. No child, neurodiverse or not, wants to go to school after spending the past hour with chaos and shouting. But particularly for neurodiverse children, a bad morning can lead to anxiety and rumination, paving the way for a bad day at school, difficulties with peers and struggling with work. So let's keep that positive mindset going and let's believe we can get through this morning and get out of the door in one piece. Let's do it!

Chapter 2

Clothes and Self-Care

Dressing

In our home, as in many households, clothes can be such a major issue. When our son was younger, he was generally okay with most types of clothes. He wasn't particularly 'fussy' or 'demanding' about what he would wear – which was a nice change of pace after having two stroppy girls who were very particular about what they liked and didn't like at a young age. But as our eldest son grew older, he was upset by clothes more and more, until the point where we are now – he will currently wear one brand of trainer, one brand of jogger and plain round-neck T-shirts (with the exception of school polo shirts once they have been washed and softened several times). That is all. It has been a long road for us to get here and, honestly, a really challenging one. We have to wear clothes all day every day, and for some children, that is just too much to handle. If you think back to Chapter 1 where I asked you to imagine how each item of clothing feels, that is a challenge our children are going through every single day.

I often think parents with neurotypical children or family members, schools – whoever – sometimes don't appreciate how difficult the dressing routine can be. For us, it's not just as simple as get dressed, get bags ready and leave for event – whether that be school, a day out, a meal, a wedding or something else. Does the following anecdote sound familiar at all?

You have prepared the night before and have all the clothes out and ready. You think they are ones your child can tolerate, and you have told your child what they are wearing tomorrow. All is fine. Then morning comes, you get your child out of their pyjamas and get underwear on to them, now socks, trousers...but the socks feel itchy so they take them off. You put the socks back on and try to wrestle them to put their top on. They now don't like the socks or the trousers (the waistband feels tight), so they take off both socks and trousers. You try to put the socks back on but get several kicks to the stomach, so you bargain with them – put the socks on and you can have a treat! Doesn't work – your child is not as fickle as you had hoped (disappointing, I know!). You wrestle the trousers back on and attempt the socks again. They wriggle and run away to hide (usually in the most hard-to-reach place possible). You again try to bargain. It doesn't work, again. Eventually, you end up pulling them out of their hiding place, where you find they have stripped all clothes off completely. The process starts again, and again, until you have some semblance of clothing on your child and only a drop of patience and sanity left. Eventually, you go to put the shoe on the right foot...while they remove the sock from the left. You put the sock back on the left, add the shoe and they have pulled the right shoe off now; right one back on and finally we are dressed – for now.

If you have managed to get through all that and get out of the door and to whatever you were aiming for on time, I applaud you because I have yet to manage it. I am notoriously late for just about everything in my life, and not through want of trying. It's not easy getting neurotypical children ready, but then add in a neurodiverse child, or children, and it becomes a whole different situation!

It is important to remember while all this is going on that your child really doesn't mean to be obstructive. What they are feeling is often overwhelming for them, yet our children have distinct issues in expressing these feelings, and so they often come out as aggression or running away. This is down to an internal process called 'fight, flight or freeze', which we all have and which helps us protect ourselves in the most dangerous situations. It helps us run from a burning building and freeze when in the eyes of a lion – but it can also be triggered by more mundane things when it works a little too well. During 'fight, flight or freeze', our sympathetic nervous system recognises there is a threat and sends signals from our brain to our body to prepare us to protect ourselves. This creates physical changes. The brain encourages the production of adrenalin, which in turn makes the heart beat faster. The blood vessels to your skin constrict while the vessels to your vital organs expand in order to help your heart get more blood – this can make you look pale. Your liver produces more glucose to give you the energy to run, the branches within your lungs expand to help you get more oxygen into your blood, and your pupils dilate to help you increase your light intake and visual acuity. All these responses are built into our DNA to help us survive in a world where we would need to protect ourselves from predators – something we rarely have to do in modern Western society.

As useful as these responses are within a threatening situation, they are not useful when they are triggered in non-threatening situations, as they are for many neurodiverse people. Often neurodiverse children will feel these physical changes in their bodies overwhelming them during unexpected times, and this is what can lead our children to *fight* us, run from us in *flight* or sometimes *freeze*. It is a biological response, and although it's hard to separate from your child or the situation, it's important to remember that it is not under the control of your child when this happens. More often than not, the person who has gone into 'fight, flight or freeze' cannot remember what has happened after their body returns to its regular tempo. This is because the centre for our memory is in the pre-frontal cortex (the front part of our brain) and this is deemed less necessary during a responsive reaction; therefore, more power is given to the parts of the brain that will help us escape (such as the amygdala) rather than the parts of the brain (such as the pre-frontal cortex) that help us with 'higher thinking' (attention, memory, executive functioning).

That is the science behind what is going on when your child is kicking you in the stomach and hiding under the table. I hope that this can help you understand that your child is not meaning to do these things – they are in a state of mind that they are not fully in control of because they often feel overwhelmed by sensory issues from clothing.

As good as it is to understand why your child is reacting in this way, however, it's also important to learn ways to help them. Here are some things I have learned throughout the years that could help you get those clothes on when you really need to.

Choose your clothes wisely

It's fairly common and somewhat natural for parents to pick out their children's clothes when shopping. At the end of the day, we are the parents or carers of these children and we know that they need jumpers in winter and shorts in summer. We are also more socially aware of what attire is expected at different events (e.g. weddings, birthday parties). But after years of buying and sending back too many outfits to mention, we have now understood that our son has very particular expectations when it comes to clothes and we may not necessarily understand what they are. Numerous times I have bought clothes believing I am doing the right thing, having a good feel and thinking he will wear them, only for him to have one feel and say no. It is soul-crushing sometimes – you think you are doing your best for your children and then you realise you really have no idea what they are battling with. Therefore, my advice would be to always take your child shopping with you. I recognise this in itself comes with a whole host of new challenges! But if you can do this once or twice a year, you can get a good grasp of what your child will and won't wear.

Last year, our eldest son wanted some new 'grown-up' clothes for Christmas. Gone are the days of PAW Patrol T-shirts and Fireman Sam hat sets, unfortunately. Keep in mind that these were Christmas presents and therefore they would, under normal circumstances, be surprises. However, knowing our son as we do, we took him out shortly before Christmas, late at night so it was less busy in the shops. We got him to choose the things he likes and we sent them off to Santa Claus to bring back on

Christmas Eve. Although this isn't perfect, it means he is seeing his clothes beforehand, he did get to pick every item, feel every fabric, run his hand along every seam and shoot down every item I thought he would like. But it meant that when Christmas Day came, he was overjoyed with his 'grown-up' clothes and put them straight on! The joy I felt that day knowing he was happy wearing them went beyond the disappointment I felt that he had seen them previously.

Once you find it, never let go!

Honestly, that title says it all. Never let go! We have found our son will only wear jogging bottoms; he finds jeans and trousers too restrictive and will not tolerate them. Over the years he has refused to wear different types of joggers, though; it can depend on the inside seams, the label, the strings in the waistband – and I'm sure there are many other things that he cannot even communicate to us. Despite this, we have found one magical pair of joggers that are soft on the inside, have a flat string in the waistband, do not have tight cuffs and are generally acceptable to him. I bet you can imagine what we did – we bought a dozen pairs of them. Mostly black as he prefers black joggers, but we do have the occasional different colour – a grey pair and a yellow pair. Most importantly, though, they are the same design again and again. They are standard and he knows what to expect from them. To continue on a theme, we also have one type of underwear he will wear and one type of socks he will wear – needless to say, we buy those in bulk too!

Again, we have done this with shoes. Our son worked so hard

at learning to tie his laces with his occupational therapist, but he soon forgot how to do them when the sessions were finished and now refuses to wear trainers with laces. So we found an own-brand pair of trainers and thankfully they make them in several different colours, so every time he needs a new pair of shoes, we go with our standard trainers in either black, blue or white. I just pray the day doesn't come when they discontinue this line of trainers, because then we will have to start the process again. But for the past five years, they have served us well.

Fastening buttons, doing up zips and tying laces are skills that can be extremely difficult for a neurodiverse child to master. A lot of neurodiverse children do not have one diagnosis in isolation; it is often very common to have additional diagnoses such as sensory processing disorder (discussed in Chapter 1), hypotonia (not having good tone within the muscles), hypermobility (being too flexible) or coordination difficulties. These are often things that even parents might not pick up on, but when you get to the point of seeing professionals, they may notice these things and work with your child to help them develop these skills.

Our eldest son was referred to occupational therapy – at the time, we knew very little about it and did not really understand how it could help us. However, when we went, we found it to be the best service we had from all his appointments. Occupational therapists worked with our son to improve his ability to tolerate different senses a little more, and they made recommendations to the school about things that would help him such as a wobble cushion and ear defenders. But they also noticed that he had low tone in his core, which was making it difficult for him to sit in an upright position, and hypermobility, which was making it difficult for him to do zips, buttons and laces. Through his sessions, he was able to develop these skills and we were given lots of advice on how to increase his tone and strengthen those muscles.

If your child is struggling with buttons or zips and cannot yet tie their laces, do not fret – there is help out there. There are books that you can get from online retailers with buttons and zips on fabric pages. These can give your child a chance to practise these skills without the pressure of it being because you are leaving the house and need it to be done quickly. These can easily be made into games, where you have a go and then your child has a go. Making learning skills into a game helps the child feel comfortable and enjoy the experience more, rather than perceiving it as a chore or negative interaction. Children are also more driven by reward-based activities than adults are (although I wouldn't say no to a chocolate biscuit as a reward!) and therefore have an inbuilt desire to do well when doing challenging games – such as learning new skills.

Choices, choices, choices

One of the barriers to neurodiverse children getting dressed can be choices – particularly if they are at an age when they are given the freedom to choose their own clothes. Choices are a wonderful thing to provide children with – they promote independence and decision-making skills – but they can also be crippling for some children. Making a choice isn't as simple as it may first appear. The brain has to weigh up the pros and cons and imagine the implications of each option. When you factor in three, four or more options, this can lead to a build-up of anxiety about getting the choice wrong and the consequences of that choice. This may seem a little dramatic – we are talking about a child choosing their outfit for the day – but even small decisions like this can be paralysing when you have too many choices.

Imagine you take your child to a large toy shop and tell them they can pick a toy – anything they like – but only one. I can bet you will spend at least an hour with your child going back and forth between their decisions. That is completely natural – not only does your child have to weigh up the benefits of having one toy, but they also have to weigh up the disadvantages of not having another toy. They go backwards and forwards between different things, not knowing what to do for the best. I'm sure it's a situation many parents have been in a number of times, and it can feel as if there is no way out when you're in it.

Children with neurodiversities can often feel this overwhelming emotion about the smallest of decisions, such as choosing clothes for the day. The key to keeping choices simple is to turn them into small tasks. Usually I do this by offering two choices at a time – for example, 'T-shirt X or T-shirt Y? White trainers or black trainers?'

Doing this breaks the task down and makes it more manageable while still giving your child autonomy over what they wear and how they express themselves. Of course, for some children, this will work well – for example, my eldest daughter who has ADHD and gets overwhelmed very quickly by clothes choices. But for other children, such as my son who will only wear one outfit, this type of technique is not needed. It's also important to factor in other issues. My son has severe sensory issues, so offering him a choice that would give him sensory overload doesn't seem fair. And my daughter is a teenager, so getting stressed over wearing the right clothes to fit in with peer groups also comes into play when making decisions about what to wear for the day.

Thank goodness for school uniform!

School uniform can be a tricky one to handle. For some children, it provides much-needed continuity – the everyday 'sameness' that they can come to expect and rely on, particularly in primary school where uniform is geared to comfort over formality. However, for other levels of education, uniform can provide more stress than we need. So what can we do about it? It is perfectly reasonable if your child has sensory issues to have these taken into account when asking the school for support. Even without an education and health care plan (EHCP), your school should be considering 'reasonable adjustments' to allow your child to attend the setting in clothes they can manage. Nobody wants to be sitting around all day in something that feels restrictive and uncomfortable.

As I have previously discussed, our eldest son will only wear black joggers and trainers. Thankfully, the school has a footwear policy that actively encourages trainers, but the trousers have been something we have had to ask for. When he was smaller, he didn't vocalise as many sensory discomforts as he currently does, and he wore regular school trousers – probably the same ones as those you have bought year after year. Yet as he got older and vocalised more sensory issues, we knew the waistband on trousers was just going to be too much. So in our clever little heads, we thought we would turn to Marks

& Spencer's specialist clothing range – super soft and no tags to compete with. As I'm sure you can imagine, our son laughed in our faces…or, more accurately, threw the trousers at us and refused to wear them. Now, there are some battles I'm willing to fight: bedtime – he needs to sleep; meal times – he needs to eat. But at school, he doesn't actually *need* those trousers to learn, and he would probably learn much better if he was comfortable – in a pair of joggers.

Therefore, joggers for school is the line we had to cross to get him into school. Something that was supported, thankfully, by his school. But it is now something that we have to consider as he moves up to high school in the next few years. Finding a school that will make accommodations and support his needs for sensory-appropriate clothing is going to be a big tick on our list of requirements. But if your child is like mine and has these sensory needs, please do know that you have a right to request adjustments: to wear trainers rather than hard-soled shoes, to wear a soft polo shirt rather than a stiff-collar shirt. These are all reasonable things to request if it means getting your child across the threshold and into the school to start their learning for the day.

If you can keep them on...

This section is honestly one of the most unusual I have ever written, so let's just say it as it is: your child may prefer to strip off…a lot! If you cannot relate to this, I commend you: you have managed to keep your child clothed for the majority of their life. However, if you *can* relate to this...well, when you know, you know. Sometimes for children with neurodiversities, having clothes on can be unbearable, as we have already discussed. As children get older and begin to learn social rules, they may understand that they need to wear clothes in certain situations (e.g. school). Sometimes they don't understand *why* they need to keep to these social rules, but they do nevertheless follow them (thankfully!). But when they get home to their safe space, the one place they know they can be unapologetically themselves and always be loved, well, this is the time they may strip off. Taking the pressures of sensory overload away, they can be themselves without restraint.

I'm sure you can see the benefit of this. When we get in from a long day, I'm sure we have all kicked off our shoes in relief more than once. For those who wear them, imagine how the freedom of removing that bra at the end of the night feels – and now imagine that restriction all over your body. To me, it makes total sense that the first thing children want to do the minute they get home is strip off!

But we all know that having naked children wandering around the house is not always ideal. There are times when your child is going to need their clothes firmly kept in place. So how do we manage that without a meltdown?

One way of dealing with this conundrum is by setting limits and boundaries. Making compromises could benefit you both and ensure everyone is getting what they need. In our house, we allowed stripping off on the proviso that underwear stays on (favourite underwear, of course!). That way, the child gets to enjoy their freedom and doesn't feel restricted, but appropriate measures are put in place so that other people in the house are not made to feel uncomfortable (we have teenage girls, remember!). If your child is younger or doesn't have the understanding to have that conversation, there are other ways to keep them clothed. One tip is getting footless sleepsuits (or cutting off the feet) and dressing your child in that but back to front. This way, the buttons or zips are at the back, and unless they perform some Houdini-style trick, it should stay on (no promises!). This is particularly useful in the colder seasons when blasting the heat 24/7 just wouldn't be feasible.

A good friend of mine has a son who enjoys stripping off a lot, particularly at bedtime. He is currently non-verbal, so she was unable to communicate why he needs to keep his clothes on. It was particularly important for this boy because he wasn't yet toilet trained, so when he removed his clothes, he would also remove his nappy. My friend tried the backwards pyjamas, she also tried specially made clothes that children aren't supposed to escape from...but her son is a genius and managed to take them both off. So she came up with an ingenious idea: she put him in a swimming all-in-one suit with a zip at the back. As if by magic, her son was able to keep his clothes and his nappy on all night without stripping off, ensuring he got better sleep and she didn't have to worry about him being cold or not having a nappy.

Another way in which stripping off can be managed is by ensuring open and honest conversations with our children at a developmentally appropriate level about their bodies and respecting others' bodies. From a very early age, we have encouraged our children to understand about their own body and their rights to only have physical contact that they want to have (e.g. 'Would you like to hug Grandma?' rather than 'Give Grandma a hug!').

I hope these bits of advice can help you mediate the nakedness in your home. Please do remember that it is not just happening in your house! I have had hundreds of conversations with parents of children who just want to strip off all the time. It is a completely normal part of parenting with neurodiverse children and neurotypical children alike.

Toileting

Toileting can be a whole issue in itself with children who are neurodiverse. This can be for a huge range of reasons, some of which I will try to cover here. But one thing to keep in mind is that it's important not to put too much pressure on yourself or your child to get toilet trained. It's a process and it isn't going to happen overnight. That being said, there are several factors to be aware of that could help you in supporting your child to toilet train when you both feel ready.

First, it's important to understand that toilet training relies on your child being able to recognise the feeling of needing to go to the toilet. The sense that helps us to understand these feelings is called interoception. Interoception tells us when we feel hungry, thirsty, cold, hot, and, in this case, when we need the toilet. Typically, our body will give us a warning signal that our bladder is filling or our bowels need emptying before it actually happens; this allows us the opportunity to find a bathroom and relieve ourselves. When we are toilet training, this gives our children the time and opportunity to understand that feeling and express it so that they can use the potty or toilet. However, interoception is a sense just like seeing, smelling, hearing, tasting and touching, and as we have previously discussed, a lot of children with neurodiversities, such as autism or ADHD, have difficulty keeping this sense balanced rather than being overwhelmed. Therefore, when toilet training your neurodiverse child, you may find they are not ready at the typical two years, or sometimes three, four or five years. And that's okay.

The second barrier to toilet training comes in the form of communication difficulties. No matter what your child can and cannot feel from their interoceptive senses, if they cannot communicate that need to their caregivers, then their needs are going to be unmet. A huge number of communication difficulties come hand in hand with neurodiversity, including speech and language difficulties and understanding difficulties. Without this ability to communicate their needs or understand directions, many children will find toilet training particularly difficult.

It can be frustrating to not toilet-train your children at the same time as their peers, but please know you are doing the best for your child and your family. To put pressure on your children to toilet-train is going to be difficult for both them and you. Toilet training too early will end up with a lot of washing, a lot of mopping up and not much progress, so waiting on their senses and their communication to develop is in the best interests of everyone, including your washing machine! If your child is non-verbal or pre-verbal (depending on which term you use), you do not have to wait until they are speaking; there are many communication tools available to help children express their toileting needs through pictures and apps. In addition to this, there is lots of help from local continence services who can support your journey and even provide larger nappies once your child begins to grow out of the standard ones. The continence team can be accessed through your GP and is a wonderful support to anyone needing it, so please do contact them if you need help.

For some children, toilet training can work and they can begin to use the potty or toilet at the expected time. However, this does not mean that there may not be difficulties down the road. It can be common for all children to forget toileting practices and routines, but this can be even more difficult if your child has difficulties with working memory or processing. For example, when we toilet-train, we tend to teach children about wiping their bottoms and washing their hands. These are both things that would be expected of children when they get to school. (This is often referred to as 'school readiness' – a combination of targets schools expect a child to have met before starting.) However, for children with working memory problems, remembering to wash their hands or, in the case of boys, remembering to lift the seat can easily be forgotten. Frustrating as this is... If you are a woman and you live with boys you do not want to sit on that seat if they have forgotten to lift it! But there are ways in which we can support children to remember these things. As I mentioned in Chapter 1, I am a big fan of having little reminder notes around the house. For our bathroom, I got the boys to join in and colour in a poster with me, in the hope that engaging them in the activity would help their memory. Our episodic memory (memory of events) can work differently from our procedural memory (memory of skill learning), so I hoped it might help it stick in a different way.

In addition to this, there can be other issues around toileting that you wouldn't even imagine. Because of the huge sensory issues neurodiverse children have, they often dislike the feeling of toilet paper. This can be the feeling in their hands or the feeling against their bottoms. Either way, adjustments can be made by altering the toilet paper or even getting some wet wipes for toilet training (please only use special toilet wet wipes; normal ones will clog up the toilet system!). Additionally, you can wipe their bottom for them – a route that we had to go down for more years than I'm willing to embarrass my child by letting you know.

But it happens; I know from many conversations that we are not the first parents to help their children wipe themselves well past the point of toilet training and we won't be the last. Do not feel guilty about it and do not worry that your child will never be able to do it; they will. These things take time and patience; your child will get there eventually, and having a supportive parent or carer along for the journey will make it a lot more manageable for everyone involved.

The final point I would like to discuss is going to the toilet at school. For some children, this can provide a barrier that is just too big and they will hold it in all day! This is most definitely not good for their little bodies to handle, and it may stop them from drinking fluids at school for fear of needing the toilet – something that can be dangerous in hot weather. The barrier here is often fear of the unknown, the child feeling too unsafe in the space to make themselves vulnerable. If the child has developed a close relationship with an adult at the school – a teacher, teaching assistant or key worker – it would be best if that person could be the one to take the child to the toilet. This gives the child a feeling of safety with someone they know and trust before they have even gone to the bathroom. It would also be helpful for the child to spend some time in the bathroom without any expectation of using the facilities at all. Just to be in the room, be comfortable with the surroundings, explore all parts of it and discuss, in an age-appropriate way, any worries they may have about their bathroom experiences at school. This could be done several times throughout the day. Learning that the bathroom is a mundane experience and doesn't have to carry lots of fear with it will help your child experience the bathroom without worries. In addition, Social Stories™ are a great way to support children with new routines and habits by gently explaining what is going to happen and what is expected of them. A Social Story could tell the story of a child who is scared of going to the bathroom and how they overcame their fear; this will leave the door open for a dialogue about your child's worries, helping them to feel safer using the bathroom in the school setting.

Teeth brushing

We have found teeth brushing such a huge challenge, and I know we are not the only ones! You can understand why, though, can't you? A child who doesn't like things that feel weird is being asked to put a minty, bristly brush into their mouth and rub it around a lot. I honestly don't think I could cope with that if I had sensory issues. But understanding why our children do not like brushing their teeth doesn't make it any easier for us as parents to ensure they have clean, healthy teeth – something that is our job to maintain as caregivers. There are some options we have been taught by our wonderful occupational therapist who explained to us how common this problem is.

First, try getting a soft-bristled toothbrush. It might not make a huge amount of difference, but it could be the start you need to get going. Additionally, there is 'flavourless toothpaste' that you can buy (we searched online). Often the complaint with toothbrushing is the strong taste of the toothpaste, whether that's minty or another flavour (sometimes they make strawberry-flavoured for children). Flavourless toothpaste can make such a huge difference in the sensory experience of brushing teeth and could be a game changer to your child's experience. If it is not a magic cure, please do not worry – it wasn't for us, although I know it has been transformational for many other families. For us, the thought of toothpaste is too much to handle, so we have to try a different tactic, which is to hide just a small amount of toothpaste within the brush and wash it with water. Our son thinks he is just brushing with water – something that he is willing to accept – but we are managing to get a little toothpaste goodness into him. Like all things with neurodiverse children, it comes down to how much you are willing to compromise to support their needs while ensuring they are taken care of, fed and clean. This works for us, but if your child struggles with brushes completely, you may need to source rubber gum brushes (available online) as these can be similar to chewy jewellery, something that children with sensory needs often enjoy using.

Bathing and recognising the need for self-care

Bathing is a tricky one because you will probably find your child either loves it or hates it! I'm sure this could be said for most children at some point, but for children who are neurodiverse, the love/hate relationship with bathing and showers can continue long after you would expect a neurotypical child to have out-grown this. For some children, the sensory feel of the water can be lovely; the feeling of wetness and water pouring may trigger their senses, and it may then be a challenge to get them out of the bath! For other children, though, the feeling of the water and the fluidity of the bath can make them feel unsettled. Thinking back to the senses we discussed in Chapter 1, this often has to do with our proprioceptive and vestibular senses. Our ability to process where our body is within the space and keep our balance can be offset by the movement of the water within the bath. For children who do not like baths, it may be worth trying other methods of cleaning such as showers. However, showers can come with their own set of issues. Many children, both neurodiverse and neurotypical, dislike showers at a young age. The water can feel harsh if it comes out fast, the noise can be loud, and showers can feel less predictable than baths.

In a similar way to learning to use the bathroom at school, it's important for your child to have time to explore the bathroom and bath without water in it, without the pressure of cleaning. Becoming more familiar with the area may help your child feel a little more confident with the support of close people to enjoy bath time. Of course, there are the age-old methods of encouraging children into the bath with the use of bath toys. There are many available and a lot of them are interactive (you know, in a safe, non-electronic, in-the-bath kind of way!). You can also now buy floating lights for the bathtub that make the whole experience interactive – bathing with one of these and the bathroom lights off can make bath time a whole new fun sensory experience that could help your child enjoy the bath more and more. If your child likes other textures such as jelly, there are packs you can get to add to a bath to make it a jelly bath! Personally, I could not think of anything worse, but my sons enjoyed climbing into a bath of jelly and playing in it for hours. I wouldn't suggest doing this often, though, as it really did leave the bath a mess!

As our children have grown older and begun to bathe on their own, it's important to remember that they may not always be aware of when they are supposed to have a bath or brush their teeth or wash their hair. Often, children who are neurodiverse will not recognise the need for bathing and cleaning themselves daily. This is not because they are older children or teens, or even because they cannot be bothered, so please do not punish them for this. While neurotypical children and teens may recognise the social consequences of body odour or bad breath, children with neurodiversities may not. They may also not recognise the cues during the day that tell us it's time to clean ourselves, such as upon waking or getting ready for bed. Often, they can be distracted and focused on other parts of their lives, completely forgetting to take a shower. As parents and carers, it is our role to step in with that friendly reminder now and again, ensuring that it is not done in a shaming or judgemental way. A tick-list somewhere they are bound to see it may help them remember to do something each day, such as take a shower. Or an alarm on their phone or even a quick text to remind them. Always ensure it is a reminder made with kindness, remembering this is part of neurodiversity – it isn't your teen just wanting to get out of showering!

Chapter 3

School/Nursery and After School/Nursery

It has reached that time when you are allowing your beautiful child off into the world. It can be a hard time for all involved. It goes without saying that letting go of your child is incredibly difficult, whether neurodiverse or neurotypical, but when your child has special educational needs, the challenge of finding a setting where they are comfortable, and you are confident, is even harder. In this chapter, I will break down the different challenges you may face while dealing with childcare or schools. I will look at things you can do to help support your child. I will also discuss the ways in which your childcare provider or school may see your child differently and how to deal with that.

Looking for the right place

Whether you have made the decision to put your child into childcare yourselves or social, economic or work reasons have made it a necessity, please be reassured that after years working in the childcare industry, I can tell you with absolute certainty that they will benefit from it. The social benefits of children's day care have been rigorously studied and governments have even developed 'free childcare' schemes for children aged 3–5 years so that all children get the benefit of improved social interaction and skills before they begin their school journey. Children are by nature social (even if they have social difficulties) and learn best from peer-to-peer relationships. No matter what skills your child struggles with, or what neurodiversity they may have, spending time with peers is important and one of the things that can help them develop their skills and build relationships.

Where they begin this journey is important, though, and you are responsible for finding the right setting for them. Let's face it, our children would likely be happy to go and play wherever there are toys and snacks! So, what is important to ask when you go and visit a new childcare setting or nursery? First, it's important to 'feel' comfortable with the setting. Your intuition can tell you a lot, and if you do not feel comfortable leaving your most prized possession within their care, then the relationship is never going to get off the ground. Take some time to have a look around the setting, chat with the staff, consider how comfortable the children appear. That's not to say that if a child is crying it should put you off the whole setting – we know children cry! But it's important to get a feel for the setting and if it fits in with you as a family and your type of parenting. Our style of parenting is very nurturing and supportive. If my child was crying, I would want to know that they would be hugged and reassured rather than expected to 'toughen up'. It's important to recognise that everyone parents differently and how the staff in the childcare setting or school conduct themselves should be in line with your parenting values.

So, there you are, looking around the nursery or the school. It feels like a nice place, but how do you know it will be a good match for your child? Now is when we grill them with the important questions. It's valuable to understand how they will approach behaviour management within the setting – are they punitive of 'bad behaviour' or do they support and encourage positive behaviour as a means to reduce 'bad behaviour'? For example, what would they do if a child was perceived to have 'naughty behaviour'? It is a fine balance of how different parents wish to manage their own children's behaviour. As parents, we (my husband and I) wouldn't want our child to get away with murder without having any consequences, but we do believe in the power of supporting children pre-emptively to ensure they know what behaviour is expected of them – as I say, it's a fine balance. These issues become more complex when you consider that our children have additional requirements that need to be supported in the setting and may not fully understand expectations and consequences. Understanding how the setting will deal with behaviours in light of this is vital; it is important to be able to trust that they will be fair but firm with your child.

Many children with special educational needs (SEN) may find it difficult to communicate their needs to you and, even more importantly, other caregivers. You may have noticed that something happens when you are a primary caregiver of a child with SEN: you get to know them so well that even without effective communication, you know what they want or how they feel – it's as if you become an extension of them. You know them best (and don't ever forget that!). But when you are handing your child over to a nursery nurse, childminder or school teacher, it's crucial to understand how they are going to be aware of your child's needs and how they will communicate with your child. Most should have methods that they use with the children already in their settings, such as visual timetables, now-and-next boards and communication cards. If the setting doesn't have methods they are already using, now is the time to ask about what methods they are going to employ to ensure your child's needs are fully met while in their care.

As discussed in Chapter 2, children who are neurodiverse can often take longer to toilet-train, and by the time your child is starting nursery or school, they may still be in nappies. This is completely typical for children with additional needs and something that you can get support with from local continence teams. Unfortunately, most 'mainstream' schools (schools that do not specifically cater for SEN children) ask that children are out of nappies when they begin school (known as school readiness). Despite this, a conversation with the setting would likely help you understand if they would be able to cater for your child's bathroom requirements. This would be considered a 'reasonable adjustment' to their policy and is an option worth exploring if you wish your child to attend that school. Most nurseries do cater for children in nappies or pull-ups, but again it's worth a conversation to help them understand how your child communicates that they need changing and how often they will change their nappy throughout the day.

As parents and caregivers, it's hard handing over the care of your child to another person, and you may have concerns. Will your child fit in? Will they make friends? How will they manage break-time? All of these are perfectly valid questions whether your child is neurodiverse or not. But having these additional needs can make this a more worrisome time than it would typically be. If these questions are stirring around in you, please do not feel you are the only parent or carer to worry – ask the staff the questions. I can almost guarantee that they have had the same question before, and they are fully expecting you to be anxious and nervous about leaving your child with them.

I am one of those mums who constantly rings and messages my children's school and nursery, and I am completely unashamed of it. Has he settled? Did he stop crying after I left him? Has she settled into lessons? Did he feel overwhelmed when they did music today? Did he (the toddler) nap? I think half the problem is I'm a huge empath, and the thought of my children (or anyone, really) being upset makes me feel what they are feeling, and I'd hate for my children to be upset and not have me there to comfort them. So I call, I email, I message on the school app, I ask for updates regularly, and I never miss an opportunity to get feedback at the end of the day. But I do it unapologetically. For the staff, my child is just one of many, but for me, they are everything and I will do whatever I can to empower them and be their voice.

One thing to be aware of when you are choosing a setting is how they plan to communicate with you. This is especially important if your child is going to have transport provided. Transport can be provided to a child when they have been given a space in a specialist school, because these are often few and far between and may involve a lengthy journey for your child. For this reason, these children are often collected on a school bus from their home and brought back to the door at the end of the day. This would be a perfect situation, except that it takes out the part of the day when you would normally see your child's teacher, which is often a vital time when you can converse and give each other feedback about how the night before or day at school has been. This isn't the only time that communication may be missed. In some schools, the teachers aren't available at the end of the day

– for example, our son's school sends each class down with the teaching assistant and asks that all questions for the teacher are sent via an app rather than at the gates in order to avoid congestion. Similarly, in nurseries, you will often get different members of the team taking your child in and bringing them out again at the end of the day. This may not be the named 'key person' for your child, depending on staffing shifts and pick-up times. All of these situations are quite common and happen in many settings, and for this reason, it is key to find out how your child's setting will communicate with you as parents and carers. Communication can be done in so many ways such as phone calls and school apps. We have also found using a printed communication book has helped us with our son settling into his setting. We complete the part about how his night and morning have been, and then we send it with him to the setting, and the staff complete how he has been while under their care. We find this way works really well for us, particularly because our son still has daytime naps and can be a bit hit or miss with eating his food. No matter which way you find to communicate with your setting, it's important to always be in contact to ensure your child's needs are completely met by all who care for them.

Let's get started!

So you have found the perfect setting for your child. Hurrah! Honestly, it's not an easy thing to do, so well done for getting this far. But now you have to get your child started there – another hurdle to overcome. First, there is getting them into uniform – we all know what an absolute challenge that can be (see Chapter 2 for more support). Next, you have to get them to actually start. There are ways in which both you and the setting can make this transition much easier for your child. Before they even go for the first time, try to get some pictures of the setting. These can be put together in a simple little book explaining what each space is and why the child may need to go into it – for example, 'This is the dining hall – you will go in here to eat your lunch.' Simple phrases like this along with pictures are what are commonly referred to as 'Social Stories' – small books (handmade is perfectly fine) that can help your child understand the process of where they will be going and the people they will be seeing.

During the COVID-19 lockdown, our family used Social Stories a lot. At the start of the lockdown, they provided a simplified way of explaining why the school was closed and why we needed to stay at home. Towards the end of the lockdown, our school provided us with new Social Stories to show the children how the school would look slightly different in the light of COVID-19 – for example, why their desks would be moved around, where they would be required to wash their hands and what the new rules were. This was also an opportunity for the school to provide our son with pictures of his new teacher: by the time the school reopened, the children had moved up years. Using simple picture-and-word descriptions like this meant we could ease our son's anxiety and give him something tangible to understand about going back to school rather than talking to him in abstract concepts that he couldn't picture.

Once your child has had a chance to look at the pictures of their new setting as much as they want to (Social Stories should be actively used, looked at and shared to aid understanding), the next step for helping your child start 'settling in' would be to go and spend some time there, with people they trust. The key here is to allow them to explore the space within the safety of their own boundaries, by having you there as their support system. This reduces the pressure of separation anxiety, and your child has the freedom of spending as much or as little time in the new setting as they wish – they are in control, because they aren't having you taken away from them. Giving them this power and freedom over their own choices will help them create a positive bond with the setting. And please don't take this to mean your child has to be verbal to let you know when they are done. As I'm sure you know as well as I do, when a child is fed up with being somewhere or doing an activity, language or no language, they will find a way to let you know time's up!

Once your child is feeling happy enough to go to the setting alone, that's where the logistical nightmare starts for many of us! As many settings will tell you, it is best for your child to start with small portions of the day and build up to something resembling a full day. In theory, this sounds great, but when you have other children to get to and from school, it can turn into a bit of a nightmare, particularly if it lasts a while. Even with these difficulties, however, I would really recommend doing it. Let your child experience the setting alone for maybe an hour at a time; build it up to two hours and then maybe three. Start to incorporate some key elements of the day into their time there, such as assembly, lunchtime, nap time (if they have one). But start with one key element and let them get used to that for a few days before introducing any others. It is important not to overwhelm your child with lots of different highly demanding tasks at first. Once your child is used to small parts of the day, build on that with your child and your setting to develop full days and eventually full weeks within the setting. Don't worry if you have setbacks during these times: it's important to remember that these are huge milestones for neurodiverse children and even small steps are really important.

Feeling anxious about school

When children, neurodiverse or neurotypical, start school or nursery, it is completely normal for there to be feelings of nerves and anxiousness. Some children have never been away from their parents or main caregivers before; some have only been cared for by family. It's a new unfamiliar place and it may cause them to have worries about it. For most neurotypical children, these fears are settled easily and can be met with love and support to help guide them into their new setting. However, it is extremely common for many neurodiversities to include symptoms of anxiety disorders. This is where the worry and anxiety become so intense and so strong that they are constant and interfere with everyday living. This is extremely common in autism, ADHD, dyslexia and other neurodiversities. It can be incredibly hard for parents to support a child with their anxiety and to see them so anxious at such a young age. Importantly, there are many things you can do as parents and caregivers to support your children to get through their anxiety and learn to understand their feelings and manage them themselves.

First, it is important to take note of what your child is feeling and recognise it as a legitimate feeling. When we diminish our children's feelings – saying things like 'It's not that bad' or 'You don't need to get upset' – what our children are hearing is that their feelings aren't right or legitimate and they shouldn't be showing those feelings. Helping your child recognise these feelings – 'I know this makes you feel scared' or 'I understand you might be worried about this' – gives them an open forum to discuss how they are feeling without fear of judgement. Often, young children and children who are overwhelmed struggle to understand how they are feeling. Using picture cards of emotions can help children name their feelings and give parents an opportunity to discuss those feelings and explain them to their children. Along similar lines, children with neurodiversities can also respond well to using zones of regulation. These are coloured zones with a multitude of emotions within them, which allow the child to indicate what zone they feel they are in, even if they cannot name their particular feelings.

Zones of regulation

Blue	Green	Yellow	Red
Sad	Happy	Frustrated	Mad/angry
Sick	Calm	Worried	Terrified
Tired	Feeling okay	Silly/wiggly	Yelling/hitting
Bored	Focused	Excited	Elated
Moving slowly	Ready to learn	Loss of some control	Out of control

When your child is anxious about going to school, using these zones or mood picture cards can open up discussion to help you talk to your child about what is worrying them.

Another way to support your child's worries and anxieties is to ask the setting to provide a key person for your child to spend time with while they are there. This is common practice in child-care settings, but often absent when children reach school age because it is expected that they can manage their emotions in a way that doesn't need such intense support. Yet a lot of children with neurodiversities do need that extra support. Having a key person to spend time with throughout the day will provide your child with a secure bond at their setting. Having a secure bond allows children to feel confident that they will be supported and they know who they can go to if they need support. This in turn can lower anxiety and help your child settle well – a win-win for everyone.

One particular way in which children can struggle with anxiety is the transition from home to school in the morning. It is well known that children who have neurodiversities such as autism and ADHD can find changes in routine difficult to manage. This can make the change from being at home in the morning to arriving at school a particularly difficult process.

For years we have struggled with our youngest daughter's anxiety. This mainly manifests itself as anxiety going into school. I often call her 'my little ball of worry'. My beautiful baby girl takes everything in life and thinks of a million different ways in which it could go wrong or could be uncomfortable for her. It is honestly heartbreaking to see. From a very young age, she struggled to get into school. I remember mornings of her running away and hiding in the house so we couldn't get her out of the door. I remember one time when I honestly felt like the worst mother in the world; she didn't want to go and I had to physically walk behind her, body to body, to make her go forward out of the door – she proceeded to grab the door handle, slump down on to the doorstep and sob that she couldn't go. Safe to say, that day we allowed her to stay home, but we know that is not the solution. This wasn't a one-off – time and time again, we have battled with her anxieties to get her across the school threshold. Even now, in high school, she continues to have significant issues with anxiety around school, and I often have to take her and walk her into the school myself – well past the time the bell has gone. But we do our best...

Getting inside the school is a huge issue for many children. These barriers, if not handled correctly, can lead to something called anxiety-based school avoidance (previously known as school refusal – this term has fallen out of favour because the children are not 'refusing'; they are in crisis and cannot get into school), where a child's anxiety and fear of school can become so extreme that they are unable even to get through the door. Neither the school nor the parents and child want that to happen, and so there are a few things that might be worth trying if your child is struggling with going into school in the mornings.

First, as we have discussed previously, getting everything ready the night before and mentally preparing your child for the morning can be a big step towards ensuring your child knows what is coming. In addition, taking the morning in small steps can help your child feel like the morning is less intimidating. Asking your child to just get up and come down for breakfast is enough, without the mention of school. You can then move on to just getting dressed and then sitting and doing something fun (for us, it's usually a morning cartoon, but you can choose a book or some toys). Moving on from this, try to make the school run something fun to do. Whether you walk or drive, use this time to create something that you only do during the morning school run – make it a story time or a time to talk about your child's favourite subject. This will give predictability to something that can feel very unpredictable for your child. It can also make it a special time for you both and something they look forward to. Try to make the time going to school something that only one or two people do (parents/grandparent/childminder), so your child can get used to who they will be going with and this doesn't give them anything else to be uncertain about. I know this can be difficult with work and shift patterns, but limiting school runs to one or two people can ensure predictability for your child – something that is so important.

Now, you might think I'm crazy or just plain old mean, but my children go to a childminder because their dad and I both work full-time. We both love our jobs and believe that it sets a good example for our children to see us in work, happy and productive. However, this means that we cannot take our younger children to school (the older ones walk). This does break my heart regularly, and I often wonder if we are doing the right thing, but for us, this works and we actually end up with fewer meltdowns this way. Because my husband works shifts, he is not always at work Monday to Friday. However, even when he is off for the day, or I don't have any early appointments or meetings, we make sure the children go to the childminder at their normal early time and get walked to school by her rather than us. Even for pick-up time, we make sure the childminder does the pick-up, and if we want to have them home early, we collect them from the childminder not long after she is home from school with them. For us, there is a clear reason for doing this. Routine. Our children thrive on routine, and often things can get more out of hand and feel more stressful when they are brought out of this routine for a special trip or Mummy or

Daddy doing the school run on the odd occasion. Ensuring this rigorous routine has helped our children know what to expect in the morning and what to expect when they come out of school – a huge benefit to them and peace of mind for us.

Another way to help support your child in the mornings if they are feeling anxious about going into nursery or school is to work with their setting to develop a 'transitional job' for them. By 'transitional job', I am referring to something that your child can do that is their responsibility once they get into their setting. This could be handing out books, ensuring all the milk cartons are ready for break-time or tidying up the school library. Having a job to go in for can give your child something to look forward to, something to give their morning purpose and a chance to start the day with some praise for completing a task that is unique to them. The job they are given obviously has to be age-appropriate. There is no point asking a three-year-old to sort out books in the library; likewise, you wouldn't ask a ten-year-old to sort the crayons into colours. Nonetheless, there is an important role in a transitional job to help your child want to come into the setting and blend the home and the setting together.

In addition to transitional jobs, there are also transitional objects that can help your child move easily from one setting to another. In general, schools do not like transitional objects, because they don't like children to bring in toys from home. However, for many years we have used transitional objects to help our son stay calm and happy at school.

A transitional object sounds fancy, but it's really just the bunny your child hugs all the time, the dolly they won't let go of or, in our case, the cuddly monkey they have taken everywhere since they were a one-year-old. When your child creates a bond with something as an infant, usually a soft toy, it is a way of them feeling secure and settled whenever that object is with them. The bond they create with their favourite object represents a close connection they have to something that they can take with them no matter where they go. When children realise that their primary caregivers can come and go and won't always be around, it can lead them to create bonds with objects that they know they can often take with them. These objects are often let go by neurotypical children as they grow older. However, for neurodiverse children, these objects can be more than just a comfort to help with the transition of learning that caregivers come and go; they can provide constant support, a never-changing object in a world that seems scary and changing all the time. When change is experienced by your child as a scary and unpredictable force, holding on to the one constant in their life can help support them to feel that everything is still and steady. Using transitional objects such as their favourite soft toy can help them manage their transition from home to school in a way that they feel safe and secure.

In our home, we have two adults, four children and Monkey. Monkey has been a part of our family since 2013 and has gone everywhere with us from then on. Our eldest son was gifted Monkey when he was one year old, and since that day Monkey has been his faithful companion. He carries Monkey from room to room; he does not go anywhere without Monkey. Monkey has been to hospital appointments, on plane rides, to foreign countries, family parties and everything in between. Most importantly, Monkey goes to school...every single day. As our son has got older, his teachers have unfortunately become more and more unhappy about Monkey going to school. We spent a year with Monkey going and sitting on the teacher's desk...so our son knew it was near but he wasn't clinging to it. Then a year of Monkey sitting on top of the board...so he could see him but didn't feel the need to cuddle him. However, last year when he moved to a new specialist school, they recognised the importance of Monkey and embraced him. Our son is now about to go into year 7 and he is taking Monkey with him. All his friends know about Monkey, and no one says a word – he's just always there. That is the difference a reasonable adjustment can make to the mental wellbeing of a child.

Ways in which settings can support your child's additional needs

Once you have finally got your child dressed, out of the house and settled into nursery or school, it's then the job of the setting to support your child's needs as best they can. There are a multitude of ways in which this can be done, but a key element of them all is communication. Ensuring an effective flow of communication between you as parents and your child's setting can make the difference between a thriving, supported child and one that doesn't feel happy or comfortable. One way to ensure effective communication is through the use of a communication book. Ready-made versions are available online or you can just use a general notebook. Either way, this allows you to share information with the setting about things that may have happened at home, how your child is feeling, if they have slept well, eaten well, if they have any worries coming into the setting in the morning. It also allows the setting to give you a picture of how your child has been during their time in their care, if they have had any problems and how these have been managed. Having this written down can also support you in recognising patterns of behaviour and what may trigger certain behaviours – for example, do they behave in a more erratic way when they have had less sleep, or do they have increased anxiety at certain points in the week? This written record of your child's everyday interactions can also help support you when going to speak with medical professionals. It can provide evidence of behaviours not just within your care but in other settings as well. This is a significant part of the diagnostic process as medical professionals often like to ensure behaviours are not just reactive to one environment but happen across the board.

When your child is at nursery or school, they may feel dysregulated at times. This could be emotional dysregulation (e.g. angry, upset or hyper) or sensory dysregulation (such as needing more or less stimulation). This is not surprising considering the significant amount of time we expect our children to be within a formal education setting. Settings should be able to provide children with ways in which they can regulate their emotions and senses in a safe way. Many have quiet calm rooms such as sensory rooms or dark tents. Many settings also have lovely cosy corners in their classrooms, usually as reading areas, that a child can use to go and take a few minutes away and re-regulate themselves. Similarly, children may crave more stimulation in the setting – interventions such as wobbly cushions and peanut balls (small bouncy balls to sit on – similar to an exercise ball) provide children with a significant amount of input to their senses. Often children who need more input to their senses can access breaks in their learning to do 'sensory pathways' (these are pathways usually in corridors that encourage jumping, hopping, bending and stretching to stimulate the senses) or to go outside and expend some energy. Settings should also provide ways for your child to express how they are feeling in a way that is accessible to the child. This could take the form of communication cards, zones of regulation, time-out passes or having a key person who knows the child well.

Chart of methods of communicating needs

Method for communicating needs	Explanation
Communication cards	Using either digital devices or small laminated cards, children can communicate their wants and needs. These are particularly useful if your child is not yet verbal or has speech and language delays that make it difficult to express their needs.
Emotion cards	Similar to communication cards, emotion cards are small cards with a simple cartoon picture of a person showing an emotion (happy, sad, frustrated, etc.) with the name of the emotion on the card. Neurodiverse children often find it difficult to name their emotions, which can cause them to be frustrated. Using pictures that show emotions can help them to label and communicate their feelings.

Zones of regulation	As discussed earlier in the chapter, zones of regulation can help children communicate their feelings using simple colours (often blue, green, yellow and red). A child may have a zones of regulation map on their desk where they can move a counter or other symbol to the zone they are currently in. This indicates to the teaching staff that they may need support.
Time-out pass	Children can be supplied with time-out passes or can be allowed to have time out of the classroom when they need it to rebalance and re-regulate their emotions or senses. This often works well with older children who are able to recognise they need time out of their learning and can manage this themselves. It is important to provide children with a space to go when they do have time out from the classroom such as a quiet room or sensory room.
Key person	Some children are provided with a key person in their settings. This is commonplace in early years settings but can also happen in other settings. Sometimes this is funded in an education plan; other times it is funded by the setting themselves. Having a person close to the child, who knows them very well and can understand their wants and needs without having to be told, can be incredibly beneficial, supporting the child and recognising their need to re-regulate before a child gets to crisis point.

There are, of course, lots of other methods that different teachers and settings may use.

Educational psychologists

(Educational psychologists are often referred to as ed psychs or EPs.)

Settings can, of course, provide many other forms of support and intervention for children. A significant amount of this can depend on the setting – its size, budget and ability to provide these interventions. Often, if a child is recognised as having 'special educational needs' (SEN), it will be arranged for an educational psychologist to provide an assessment and report. An educational psychologist report will be based on a range of tests and assessments and will be able to help you understand how your child learns and barriers they may have to their learning. Educational psychologists can also diagnose certain neurodiversities such as dyslexia, dyscalculia, dysgraphia and other specific learning difficulties (SLD). However, many children do not need a specific diagnosis to benefit from an educational psychologist assessment. As part of the assessment, the educational psychologist will provide a report with detailed recommendations for interventions and supports to be put into place in the educational setting. From this report, they will support the setting in implementing this advice to best serve your child.

Education health care plan (EHCP)

(Also known as IEPs (Individual Education Plans) in America. Other countries may use different terms.)

If, despite all the efforts of the teachers, your child is behind academically or needs more support in a social and emotional context, they can get an education health care plan (EHCP). This is a document that reports all your child's difficulties as well as their strengths. It will include recommendations from an educational psychologist and discuss ways to support your child in their setting. It will also have specific and measurable targets for your child to achieve throughout their time in nursery and education. The benefit of having an EHCP is threefold. First, your child is recognised as needing support over and above what the general classroom/nursery offers. This can help your child access extra academic and socio-emotional support and can help teachers understand the difficulties your child is experiencing. Second, an EHCP is a legal document; once your child receives one, their setting is legally obliged to provide the support for your child outlined in the plan – without excuses. Third, the EHCP is reviewed every single year in a big meeting involving everyone who supports your child or has an interest in their education and development. As parents, you are invited to participate in these meetings and discuss any changes you think need to be made to the plan. This is beneficial because the needs of children will change over time as they grow and develop. This can be particularly significant when a child enters their tweens and teens and the social pressures on them become a lot more intense. Please know that you do not have to have a diagnosis to get an EHCP – as long as you can provide evidence that your child has educational needs over and above what is typical for their age.

The EHCP process can be a daunting one, but there are lots of support agencies out there to access help. Often other parents can provide information and support, in addition to the official channels such as information and advice services run by local councils. Generally speaking, the process should be 20 weeks long (although this can vary if you apply close to or during the summer holidays). When you apply, you can either do this through your setting (they may have suggested applying for a plan) or you can do it yourself as parents – do not be put off by this. This may seem scary, but you can apply by sending a simple email outlining the reasons you think your child needs an EHCP and attaching whatever supporting documents you can. You may hear scaremongering from other parents or settings claiming parent applications are never accepted – they are.

Once you have submitted your request, or your setting has submitted their request, you have a little wait. The application will go to a panel that decides if your child meets the requirements to do an assessment. This has to be done within the first six weeks after applying. Once you have your 'agree to assess', this is where the main body of the assessment will take place. You should be appointed an EHCP coordinator from your local council's special educational needs and disabilities (SEND) department who should keep you apprised of what's going on throughout the process. The council will write to anyone involved with your child for information they feel is relevant to the application. They will appoint an educational psychologist if they feel your child's needs warrant an assessment (depending on your child's neurodiversity). They will also ask you for your views about your child and your child's own views – which you can help them write about if needed. Once they have everything they need, your EHCP coordinator will put all this information together and present it to another panel consisting of relevant professionals. These are the people who will make the decision to give your child an EHCP or not, and they will decide how much funding will be attached to the EHCP. This decision should be made by week 16 of the process. If, at this point, it is agreed that your child needs the support of an EHCP, the council will write out a draft plan and send it to you as the child's parent/main carer. You have two weeks to look at this and recommend any changes you feel need to be made. You have a right to change things on the EHCP, and your opinion matters, so have the confidence to do so. At this time, you also have the opportunity to name a setting or school. This could be the setting or school your child already attends, or it could be another setting you feel would be more suitable for your child. The setting will then be consulted, and they have another two weeks to either accept or decline your child; generally, you would only be declined if they felt they could not meet your child's needs. This brings the total process to 20 weeks from application to the final draft being written up.

We were told for many years that our child would benefit from extra support, but he needed an EHCP to get that. We were also told that to apply for an EHCP, you first had to have an ed psych report and the waiting time for this through his setting was two years. Eventually, struggling with how to help our son, we decided to apply ourselves and give it a try. We sent a detailed email explaining why we felt our son needed extra support and the difficulties he had. We sent attachments of all his diagnostic reports, speech and language therapy reports, occupation therapy reports and school reports. And we waited...

A few weeks later, we were informed that the application

had been accepted. Phew – first hurdle over. The SEND department at the council then appointed an educational psychologist who did his assessment within two weeks – not two years! His report, the school's feedback and our evidence were all put together and taken to a panel. Our son was deemed to need an EHCP and was approved for one.

Obviously, I am not saying every application will be as smooth sailing as ours. But what I do want to make clear is how important it is to give it a try if you feel your child needs it. You are their main cheerleader, their one true supporter and the best advocate they will ever get. You are their voice where they don't have one (metaphorically or actually!). Don't let fear of the unknown stand in the way of your child making the best progress they can and being their best selves.

Sometimes it can feel as if the process is never going to end, and sometimes it can feel as though you are the only one fighting for your child. But I can tell you, it is worth it and it is possible. Ignore the naysayers, ignore the critics and those who do not support you in getting the best for your child. If, at any of the points within the EHCP process, you do get declined (at the six-week panel or the 16-week panel), you have the right to appeal the decision and ask them to look at it again. There is support out there to help you do this, so you are not alone, and you can contact other parents who have been in the same position. Find those parents (usually hanging around Facebook forums) and lean on them; they have been where you are, and they have walked the same path and fought the same fight. They are your village.

After-school meltdowns

More often than you would believe, children with neurodiversi-ties, whatever they may be, present as 'typical' children in their daily setting. You will often hear the phrase 'Well, they seem fine here!' It's a gut-wrenching phrase because, on the one hand, you want your child to be settled and happy within the setting; on the other hand, you know that your child is only appearing 'fine' because they are holding it all in. Many neurodiverse children have a wonderful talent for masking their behaviours. Masking is a type of defence mechanism that is often used when people do not know how to act within a situation or feel they need to hide parts of themselves for fear of not fitting in or repercussions. For children, this can present as appearing to be 'okay' with school or looking as though they are coping. Internally, however, they could be struggling significantly with their emotions and feeling very dysregulated.

Masking is particularly common in girls with autism, and often this can lead to a significant under-diagnosis rate for girls compared with boys. Girls tend to be able to understand social cues better, and although they don't naturally know how to use these because of their difficulties, they can recognise what social cues others are using and often mimic these to appear as though they are coping. This amount of effort that is put into social situations, over and above what a neurotypical person has to put in with their natural ability to be social, can cause exhaustion and stress to build up to a point where the child can no longer mask or hold it all in. It's important to remember that this happens not only with autism but with all neurodiversities. Trying to live as a neurodiverse person in a neurotypical world that is not accommodating is exhausting and frustrating, to say the least.

As a child, I struggled significantly with dyslexia. My primary school recognised it but told my parents they couldn't get me tested because it wasn't something that was done then (we're talking early 1990s!). When I got to high school, I managed to pass the 11+ by some miracle and I went to a private school. They (or one English teacher specifically) told me I was lazy and I just couldn't be bothered to look up the words in the dictionary. But I wasn't lazy; I was struggling. I didn't understand how people looked up words in the dictionary if you know what the first letter is but don't know any more. We didn't have laptops to do our work on, and a PC at home was a rare thing, so all our work was handwritten. For years, I lived with big red marks all over my work and being told I wasn't good enough. Within a week of starting college, a teacher noticed me struggling; she arranged an ed psych assessment and bam! – I had all the support. Extra time in exams, understanding from teachers, extra pastoral support. At university, I had an academic coach and a laptop provided with speech-to-text programming.

For years, I sat in my academic bubble feeling not good enough, but what I recognise now is that the neurotypical world was what wasn't good enough. They didn't see me for who I was or support me where I was. I was made to feel less than to fit into school and I would bury that deep inside my psyche for years.

One thing we know about masking is that the emotions have to go somewhere. Some children are like me and may hold them in for years until they are adults and it finally all comes out to some poor therapist! But most children will hold them in for a day or a week, and then they will burst out all over you like spilling a bowl of tomato soup! The reason this happens is because our children, on the whole, feel safe with their parents or carers. They know that if they are to flip out, cry, scream, shout or throw, they may get in trouble, but they will always be loved. We are their meta-phorical comfort blanket. Your children coming home and sud-denly changing from the nice, happy child the teacher reported at the end of the day to the angry, sobbing child in front of you is the highest compliment they can give you – they feel safe. And yes, it's exhausting and loud and frustrating, but this is what they have needed to do throughout the day – the build-up of emotions should have been let out in little bits – instead, it has mounted up into an enormous outburst.

There is an analogy used in neurodiversity circles called 'the Coke bottle analogy'. Imagine your child is a little bottle of coke, all calm and still when they wake up in the morning. They have to get dressed and go through their morning routine and they don't like the feel of their clothes...so the Coke bottle is given a shake. They get to school and they struggle to get through the door because they are anxious...the Coke bottle is given another shake. They go up to class and everything is fine, but then the teaching assistant takes over the class because the teacher has to do some paperwork. Your child doesn't know the teaching assistant well and feels unsure talking to them...so the Coke bottle gets a shake. It's lunchtime and your child goes out to play. They are having fun with their friends when someone bumps into them running. They are not hurt but it shocked them...the Coke bottle is shaken again. Finally, it's the afternoon, and your child is expecting it to be science but the teacher wants to give them a fun afternoon so they do another activity. This is different from what your child was expecting and it unsettles them...so the Coke bottle is shaken again.

Your child walks out of school and into your arms... They take the lid off their Coke bottle and POW! Emotions flying everywhere.

So, if you are a parent of a child who, you are told, is 'fine at school' but you see a different story at home – I see you. I see how people saying that makes you feel little; I see how you are made smaller and made to question yourself. I believe you.

Trust

The relationship between parents/carers and their child's school is such an important one. Your child is going to be spending six and a half hours a day in their care, and they are going to be in charge of not just their education but their personal care, their social development, their understanding of rules and boundaries and their ability to manage interpersonal relationships.

Trust is earned and trust is a two-way relationship. Building a relationship with your child's teachers, special educational needs coordinator (SENCo) and headteacher is vital in ensuring the right support for you and your family. Diagnosis or not, you have every right to speak to your child's SENCo, to discuss your child's needs and request support. Building a positive relationship should mean that when there are any issues you may not feel comfortable with, you can discuss them in a constructive way to advocate for the needs of your child first and foremost. As a rule, I tend to keep most communication to emails to ensure there are records of conversations. When not using email, try to make notes with dates about conversations and support that has been offered. This can help you as you move through the education system.

What if it all goes wrong?

For some children, school can become too difficult and too challenging. We have dealt with this ourselves, and it is draining both for your child and for you. Please do not beat yourself up, and please do not blame your child. Getting them back into education is important – but so is their mental health. Just as we can take time from work when our mental health dips, so should children be able to. Particularly in this post-pandemic time when so many children are struggling, have patience, work with the school, report the absences every day and do what you can to support your child.

Sometimes, a school setting is not the best place for a child – neurodiverse or not. Many parents choose to homeschool their children. This can be a wonderful step for both children and parents to explore the topics they enjoy and go at a pace that suits them both. However, homeschooling does require a lot of dedication, and having the onus on you to educate your child can create a divide between you and your child, as they now see you as an educator rather than a parental figure. There is lots of support out there for homeschooling parents, and many local colleges can support children to get their qualifications in Maths and English at GCSE level.

Chapter 4

Food

Eating can be a wonderful, enjoyable experience for many. Often, we share meals, share conversation and make eating into a social activity. Many holidays and religious celebrations involve food – for example, Thanksgiving, Hanukkah, Christmas, Eid and Diwali. For families and individuals across the globe, food can be the glue that binds them and encourages their social interactions.

From when we are very young, mealtimes are social situations. We are encouraged to eat together as families, children at school eat together at tables in lunch halls, and as we grow into adults, we often meet friends for lunch or synchronise our lunch break with a co-worker's.

Therefore, when we think about food in terms of a child who may have difficulties, we can understand where obstacles may arise, not just with the food itself but also with the social aspects of eating a meal.

Issues around food are extremely common in the neurodiverse population, particularly for children with autism spectrum disorder (ASD) but also for other individuals who have other neurodiversities. So, if your child is struggling with mealtimes, you are not the only one out there. You may watch all the 'perfect parents' (by the way, there is no such thing!) on Instagram and

Facebook, with their children eating five vegetables a day and tucking into their avocado-on-toast at the weekend, and feel as if you are doing something wrong – but I promise you, you're not.

There may be many feelings that come up when trying to deal with a child who refuses food. The first can be the initial frustration. If your child has got to a stage of food refusal, it will be a confusing time for both them and you. Often young children go through a phase of food refusal and come out of it a few weeks later, and that is a completely typical part of child development. Short bursts of food refusal in this way are commonly a way for your young child to assert their independence and demonstrate to you that they have an opinion that differs from yours. Exploration of their own opinions is truly a good thing, although it is frustrating when a child is throwing their mashed potato back at you. However, when a child is truly refusing food because of other issues, there can be confusion – is it because of typical development or are there other issues? – and thus frustration with your child may occur. Recognising the underlying reason behind a child's food refusal can be the first step to understanding your own reaction to it. When we can recognise that our children not eating the food we have prepared is not a slight, and is not a demand for more independence from them, we can balance our reaction to be more understanding of their needs.

Another common feeling among parents is sadness and worry for their children. This is completely understandable, and I have been there many a time through the years. When children are refusing food to the point that it makes them unwell, there is a feeling of despair and worry for your child that can overwhelm you. If you are in this position, there is help, I promise. There are support services, there are nutritional supplements and there are better days ahead.

In this chapter, I will discuss some of the issues relating to food issues in neurodiverse children and the ways this can impact their health. To counterbalance this, I'll then talk about ways to manage food aversion and handle eating on a limited diet in different settings. As you know, with all the advice in the world, all we can do is try. What works for one child may not work for another, and what works one time may not work another time. Be patient – with your child and with yourself.

Aside from the social expectations of food, there are also multiple reasons a child may struggle to eat their food or go off a particular food. First, as we have already discussed, impairments in the sensory systems are common in the neurodiverse population, so when we think about food, we need to consider the following things.

Sense considerations

Consider...	Which sense?	What to think about...
Taste	Gustatory	How does the food taste?
Texture	Tactile	What does it feel like out of the mouth? What does it feel like in your mouth?
Smell	Olfactory	How does it smell?
Sight	Visual	What does it look like? What does the packaging look like?
Sound	Auditory	What does it sound like when you touch it or eat it?
Memories		Does it trigger a specific memory?
Association		Does the child associate this food with a place or time?

Let's take a look at each of these components and break them down a little. The most obvious one is taste. How a food tastes has a massive impact on whether or not a food will be eaten. Studies have shown that children's palates are not as developed as adults', and therefore it may be harder to please them with tempting foods. There is also some research to suggest that children are more likely to develop a preference for sucrose or sweet flavours younger, and then go on to develop their taste for sour, salty or bitter foods as they move through their adolescent years.[3] Children will often taste something once and be sure that they do not like that food. But as the tastebuds develop throughout childhood and adolescence, it's important to encourage children to reapproach foods and try again, even if it's only a bite!

There is also the question of how the food feels, and this isn't just when we are eating it but when we hold it or touch it to eat it. The first step with many foods is picking up the item itself (sandwiches, crisps, rice cakes, etc.). If a child is so sensory averse that they cannot even bring themselves to touch the item of food, then no matter what it tastes or smells like, they are not going to pick it up. However, if they can touch the food and pick it up, there is a second hurdle in the texture category that we have to manage – food often changes texture once it enters our mouth. The texture they feel with their hands may not be the same texture that they feel with their tongue. For a young child, this can be quite scary and can put them off trying other new foods. On the flip side, the feeling of a particular food may be really enjoyable and may trigger an under-responsive sensory system. In this scenario, you may find your child eating the same food again and again. Often this is not because they are hungry but because they crave the sensory input the food gives them in their mouth.

Time and time again, I have been told about children who crave one particular food repeatedly. This is not usual with children who have restricted food, as is often the case with neurodiverse children. However, more often than not, the food is something that has a particular crunch to it – crisps are often a fan favourite and sometimes crackers or rice cakes. Children can get fixated on one particular food. When you tie this into the other senses too, this food often has to be the same flavour (e.g. ready salted crisp) and the same brand. This level of 'sameness' provides comfort and security while also giving them the sensory input they know they will enjoy.

Following on from texture is the smell of the food. I'm sure a common experience is enjoying the smell of a meal being cooked as it drifts through the house. For some, this is a wonderful smell. For me, waking up in the morning to the smell of a beef joint in the slow cooker is one of the best smell moments I can remember! However, for others – those with sensory dysregulations – the smell of food can be incredibly off-putting and overwhelming, to the point where they cannot handle being around the smell. Not all individuals smell the same, and what is enjoyable for one person may be an olfactory offence to the next. It's important to remember that as we bring food towards our mouth, its smell is brought closer to our nose, and the combination of both can often trigger negative feelings and food refusal.

The visual perception of food is something we can all relate to. When a food doesn't look appetising, psychologically it's harder for us to eat it. Think about *I'm a Celebrity...Get Me Out of Here!* and their food trials. Everything they give the celebrities is safe to eat, but the appearance of the food makes a lot of us recoil in disgust at the idea of eating it. For children with issues around food, this can be the case for the foods that typically many of us would find appetising to look at. Often these are foods that have a sauce or are wet – the appearance of food like this can trigger a fear in the child of the way the food is going to affect their other senses. Sometimes, this can be the colour of the food. Many times, children with food issues struggle with foods of different colours, and you may find they prefer to follow a diet of 'beige food', something common with many children dealing with similar issues. Pasta, bread, rice, rice cakes and, of course, chips (fries)...these are just some of the bland 'beige' foods that many children who struggle with food will eat. However, the visual perception of the actual food is not the only issue. Some children with neurodivergence really struggle with changes, and this can include the way things look. When brands change their packaging, it can have a huge effect on children who are used to the way something looks and can cause them to refuse the food inside simply because of the change in the look of the outer product.

Finally, food itself can take us back in place and time to another day. Food holds so many memories. I'm sure a lot of us could think back to times when we've had a meal with family or friends, and that meal or that food can bring back positive associations.

Take a minute and think back to a time you have sat around a table and enjoyed a meal. The good feelings this brought, the happy memories, the positive connections, the laughter and the good conversation. Can you put yourself back into that moment? Can you smell the food – a roast maybe? A Sunday morning fry-up? A Nando's?

We all have those foods that can transport us to another time and place, and it's a wonderful thing that they do that. However, if food has always been difficult for your child, and many of the times they have tried food have been stressful or unpleasant for them, those memories can be unpleasant. The happy times you recall could – for them – trigger memories of overstimulated systems, of touching unpleasant textures and tastes, of feeling pressured into eating. When we consider what an important part of social culture eating is to many of us, not being part of that, through no fault of our own, could trigger feelings of isolation and anxiety. These are, of course, things we hope to avoid as parents, but with the best will in the world, occasionally a mealtime may become stressful. This isn't to say that all mealtimes should be fairies and daffodils, but it does serve to remind you that your fond memories around family meals and enjoyable foods may not be the same as they are for your children.

In this next part, I want to talk to you about two concepts that you may not come across before but which to me, as a parent of a neurodiverse family, feel like two of the most important things you can know about your child – particularly in relation to their eating habits.

The first is 'interoception'. Interoception sounds like a complicated thing, but really it is one of our senses. It's not talked about as often as the big five (taste, smell, sight, sound, touch) but is just as important. Interoception refers to our ability to feel the things inside us. It is most likely something that we all take for granted. Can you feel when you are hungry and then full? Can you tell when you are thirsty and when your thirst is quenched?

Can you recognise how it feels to be tired or rested? For most neurotypical people, these feelings, and the ability to explain them, come as second nature. However, for some individuals, particularly with neurodivergent patterns of thinking, these feelings, and the ability to recognise them, do not come naturally. Therefore, when our children feel hungry or full, thirsty or quenched, sick or queasy, they do not know what these feelings are or how to do anything about changing them.

For example, typically when we get hungry, we are able to tell from messages sent from our stomach to our brain. Our brain would then direct us to resolve that uncomfortable feeling by eating some food. However, when a person has a poor interoceptive sense, they do not recognise the messages saying they are hungry. They may then become uncomfortable, irritable and overwhelmed – yet they don't know how to fix it. This lack of interoceptive understanding can be a huge barrier to understanding what is making a child unhappy – particularly if they are pre-verbal or non-verbal.

Hand in hand with interoception is our second concept – alexithymia. Alexithymia is the inability to describe our feelings both emotionally and physically. As you can imagine, these two concepts go hand in hand, because even if your child can recognise what they are feeling (e.g. hunger), being able to label that feeling and name it out loud is a whole other skill. It's been found in research that up to 50 per cent of individuals with autism spectrum conditions have alexithymia, and it can account for the difficulties in both interoception and emotional sensitivity.[4]

Have you ever asked your child 'What's wrong?' only to be met with a grunt or a shrug? Times when they are not happy and something is bothering them, but neither you nor they can put a finger on it. Alexithymia may be the reason for this. Understanding our complex emotions and feelings is a difficult skill to master and one that not all of us have. In these situations, be patient, be kind and give love. They may not be able to tell you what is wrong – but the love, patience and kindness will support them through whatever is causing them distress until they are out the other side. They may never know what was bothering them, but they will nonetheless feel the security of having a safe place to have those emotions.

Let's eat!

Now that we have covered some of the things that may interfere with your child eating, let's take a look at how to actually get them eating. For parents and caregivers, it's a really difficult balance. We want to respect our child's needs, their emotions, their ability to tolerate certain senses...yet we also want them to be healthy and happy, eating nutritious meals. Sometimes this balance is a tightrope between two parts of your heart, and it's okay if sometimes you don't know if you're doing the right thing for your child. We all struggle sometimes to know what to do for the best. There is no manual on parenting a neurodiverse child; if there were, it would tell you there is no right or wrong way – just your best. And I can tell you now, this process is not a 'quick fix' for eating issues; this is a new way of living with food and a new understanding of incorporating any type of food-related activity into your home, your family and your child's life.

So, let's start with the basics. Many children have set foods that they will accept – as previously mentioned, this is often known as the beige food diet. If your child is neurodiverse, or you suspect they may be neurodiverse, try to think of these foods as your 'safe foods', your fallbacks in case they won't eat other items. Don't use these foods as treats or rewards (even if they aren't the healthiest); keep them as staple foods that your child has access to no matter what. Their ability to stay in a good relationship with food relies on these foods being stable within their lives and being a positive thing, not something that can be taken away for poor behaviour or poor eating in other areas.

Recognise that food issues are not fussiness, stubbornness or pig-headedness. Your child's relationship with food could be a complicated one, and they need space and compassion to help support them. Seeing your child's behaviour as fussiness minimises the physical and mental pain they may feel around food and may lead to even further food issues, as well as a lack of trust in the person providing their food. Building trust between yourself and your child around food is a vital part of the process of getting more different foods in their diet. It is for this reason that I strongly discourage tricking or coercing your child into eating foods that they are not aware of. I'm sure we have all tried hiding vegetables in something, giving a vegetable finger instead of a fish finger – anything to get a few more vegetables into their diets. However, not being open and honest with your child about their food is only going to plant seeds of distrust. So, from this point on, tell them what you have given them, and explain to them why it's good for them and why you would like them to eat it. But never force them; it is their decision to make.

One of the best methods for introducing children to new foods and experimenting with food is to allow them to be around the food with zero pressure of having to eat it. This may sound strange at first, but if you can get your child comfortable enough around a food for long enough, they will become desensitised to it and may begin to tolerate it as an eating food in the future. This process is often referred to as sensory integration therapy, and it can be done really easily at home without anything fancy other than you, your child and your time.

First, remember this process is lots of small steps, and each step can take as long as your child needs. Some children may go faster than others, some children may take longer on one step compared to another, some children may go backwards at times... all of these things are fine. Go at your child's pace and be patient.

For young children, a very first step can be just playing with toy food. Enjoying make-believe with plastic or wooden food that doesn't have offensive smells or textures can introduce them to the world of foods in a safe and comfortable way. In older children, if they can manage a supermarket, you might want to try taking them along shopping to pick the foods off the shelf – with no pressure to have that particular item as a meal. If shopping is a no-go for other reasons, ask them to help you stock the cupboards at home. This act of being around food without any pressure to consume it can help children feel more comfortable around the food before they actually try it. This stage can be continuous throughout the process and doesn't have to be something that is forced or structured – it can be anything you do with your child around unopened, packaged or play food. Regularly incorporating this into their play or home routine will build up a tolerance to be around foods in a safe way and may also open the door for conversations, questions and explanations about food – if you're lucky!

The next stage of sensory integration is to be around foods that your child may struggle with – but without any pressure to eat them. This can be broken into many small steps, and it's at your and your child's discretion when to move up through the stages. Within this stage, the main aim is that they can be around a food for a small amount of time. To start this off, you could simply ask them to look at the food you are eating, share a table with you while you're eating it or step into the kitchen when you're cooking it. The smallest steps are still huge leaps, keeping in mind all the sensory information that just being in a kitchen cooking food will involve. From this step, you could move up to having the food at the table with them. Make them their meal as normal – plain nuggets, pasta, whatever they choose. Keep mealtime as typical as possible, but add one extra separate bowl next to your child's plate with a very small amount of the new food. This step is simply for them to tolerate being around the food, and there should be no question of the food being eaten. It is simply there, in the bowl, just to look at.

If your child can tolerate this for a short while, this is an amazing achievement! Well done to them, and well done to you! These things aren't easy, and they do take time, but you are getting there!

So now we are close, in physical proximity anyway, to having a new food. We have worked on gaining confidence near foods and tolerating being around the food, and it's time to move on to the next step – experiencing the new food. This bit can feel very difficult and can take much longer, with a significant amount of pushback. This is completely typical, and it's okay to slow down or stop at any point – we need to take this at the child's pace and respect their autonomy. This sentiment goes not just for accepting when verbal children say they do not want to do more, but also recognising non-verbal communication that a child doesn't want to proceed any further. This is just as important for those who are pre- or non-verbal.

Once your child is comfortable around the food and being in the presence of the food, you can start exploring the idea of touching the food – as before, with no pressure to eat the food. But a small touch of the finger to feel what the texture is like, to feel the stickiness of pasta, the gain of rice or the wetness of the sauce. The food should still be in a separate bowl, and the child should be fully aware that they are not expected to eat any of the food or even touch it if they don't feel comfortable. As before, it's about going at the pace of the child and what they are comfortable with. Traumatising them with pressure and disappointment is not going to get them eating more food. The choice has to be theirs, built with the confidence and support that you can provide them to realise it is safe. If they will feel some of the food, even the smallest drop against their finger, heap the praise on. What they have just done is the equivalent of climbing a mountain in their head, and it should be celebrated in this way too! Clap, cheer, jump up and down, and tell them how proud you are from your heart. They are trying so hard to do things that do not come naturally to them and do not feel comfortable for them. But by doing this, they will be able to open their palate to a wider variety of foods and stay healthier throughout their lives – something we will go on to talk about at the end of this chapter.

After a touch to a finger, and the mountain of praise that comes with that, work your way forward. Can they touch it some more? Could they touch it to their lips? Talk about the texture – what they like about it and what they do not like about it. Enjoy spending this time talking about foods, discussing the good and the bad and everything in between. Allow them the time, space and attention to feel their feelings and be open with you about them. Accept how they feel, if they can tell you, and avoid dismissive language like 'Oh, it's not that bad' or 'It's only a little bit'. Try to develop a relationship with food for your child that is positive and built upon a foundation of respect for how food makes them feel.

Eventually, if they can get to this point, then they can try a small bit. Just a tiny amount. Still on a separate plate, still not the focus of the main meal and still pouring on that praise like never before. If your child has reached this stage with a food, they are amazing and so are you. But this is the make-or-break part, I am sorry to say; it is at this point of no return that they are going to either like or dislike the food – and that is completely their decision to make, as it is for all of us. You may have a child who at this point likes the food (hurrah!) and will then go on to incorporate it into their diet. This is amazing, not just because it widens their current food palate, but it also teaches them that they can do this process and they do have the strength to try new things. But you may have a child who gets to this point, or points before this, and cannot continue. That's okay too! To even try this journey is a challenge, and for many neurodiverse children, it is a challenge you are likely to be working with them to support for a very long time. And that's okay.

Now for the bad news: the process we have just been going through...well, it needs repeating with every food you want to try to get your child to tolerate. I did warn you at the beginning that this wasn't going to be a quick process! But it is so worth it. When your child will eat no more than three foods and, suddenly, they are picking up a fourth and eating it, there is no more joy than knowing you have supported your child to get to that point.

Your child's relationship with food may be a complex one, but it's a journey and a relationship that you can be part of by supporting them in any way they need through the process. Unfortunately, as we have previously discussed, many things can change about how a food is received by a child with food issues. These feelings can be transient and change over time – they can love a food one day and hate it the next – and you may have to start the process again and again with different foods at different stages in your child's life. This is not uncommon at all and is something your child will lead the way on always. As I've discussed, one of your main roles is to be their cheerleader, their confidant and their trusted person. If a child tells you they no longer want to eat that food, be accepting of this, understand and try to get them to discuss (if they can) their reasons. If they refuse food, put a positive spin on it: 'Okay, we're not eating that today. That's okay, maybe we can eat that next time we are cooking it.' Lower the expectations and increase the praise.

For our son, we have four main foods. Bread (Warburtons in the orange packet), which he has toasted with only Vitalite dairy-free spread (because of allergies). Bread (again!) which he has untoasted, and uncut, for his packed lunch. Plain sponge cakes (Asda – no others), raspberry and apple cereal bars (Goodies) and micro-chips (McCain). That is his diet. But that's okay because he is safe and comfortable with those foods. Occasionally, we will work up the ladder of including a new food and he will tolerate something else for a while – right now, this is chicken poppers (only if we get Sainsbury's own). But we know this may not last, just like the plain chicken breast he ate a few years ago didn't last, or the small grab bags of Fridge Raiders chicken didn't last. However, we keep trying, we keep encouraging and we keep being immensely proud of how hard he tries to develop his diet.

Our son isn't the only child going through this. I've worked with children who will only eat sausage rolls or cucumbers by the dozen. I've known neurodiverse children who only want to eat pizza for every single meal or eat just ketchup sandwiches. To each of those children, their meal choices have made sense and felt right. To each of their parents trying to support their children to get something more into their diet, I see you, I am you and I know how hard you are trying.

In the next section, we're going to discuss ways in which we can help and support our children when eating in different scenarios, such as eating at school, eating out and managing people's unwanted opinions.

Eating at nursery and school

So, let's start with nursery or school. As a child grows, it's likely that they will attend some kind of formal childcare or education establishment. It is also highly likely that your child will need to have a meal in their setting at some point. As a parent, it can be really difficult to manage your feelings about this while also reassuring your child that they are going to be as supported at nursery or school as they are within their home environment. The honest truth is that they're most likely not. I do not say this to bring you down or send you into a panic, but as a parent or carer to a young child, you are their rock, their pillar of strength. No other person is going to look out for your child in the way you are, and that's okay, but it is important to keep it in mind.

Therefore, when arranging for your child to eat at nursery or school, be aware that you are not going to be there; manage the expectations for both your child and their careers. Your child does not have to try weird and wonderful foods from around the globe in an educational setting where they are not comfortable and do not have you there as their cheerleader. Arrange a meeting with the childcare setting or school and let them know what your child will and won't eat, and ask for this to be passed on to the catering staff. If you think your child will eat some foods made by the setting, encourage your child to partake in mealtimes as much as they feel comfortable. However, if you feel your child is not going to manage the foods prepared by the setting, that's okay – not every mealtime has to be a battle to be won. It is perfectly okay to provide your child with a packed lunch with all their favourite safe foods. It's okay that Jack's mum sends him with avocado and spinach (go, Jack!) and Ava's mum sends her with a rice and bean salad (go, Ava!), and it is always okay that your child is having their same four beige foods in their pack-up, day after day. You are doing the best for your child and that is what is important – at the end of the day, a child eating is better than a child not eating. The old wives' tale of 'they will eat when they are hungry' is just that – an old wives' tale. Your child may not eat when they are hungry if they are not provided with the right foods; they may wait all day until they get home to be given something safe. They may spend their days in class hungry and unable to concentrate. For this reason, I have always used the mantra 'food is food'. I can work on incorporating the right vitamins and minerals, and I can work on balancing carbohydrates and proteins, but I cannot allow my child to go hungry for the sake of a slice of toast cut the right way – no battle is worth that.

Eating out at restaurants

Now at this point, I'm not going to lie to you and say eating out is going to be easy and you are going to have wonderful fancy meals out all over town with your children in tow...because, honestly, how many of us would do that with children anyway? Eating out may be one of the hardest eating challenges you will come across. It is a new situation, often with lots of sensory experiences to absorb, from lighting and sound to smells and atmosphere. If you do not regularly eat out, it can be out of routine for your child, and that in itself can lead to it being a difficult trip. But that is not to say you will never eat out. It can happen.

My first recommendation is to find a place that you feel will meet your needs for a meal while also being mindful of the sensory experience your child may have there. Go and check the venue out beforehand or check on Google to see if there are any pictures. How is the lighting? Do the tables look well spaced or does everyone get packed in? Can you sit in corners or is it all open plan? (Booths are great!) Once you're happy and settled on a place, give them a call. Explain your child's world to them; most staff will not have had any training on neurodiversity and how they can help a family. When you explain to them, that may be the first time they have realised they have the means to make your experience at the restaurant manageable. If your child is going to need a quiet space in the restaurant, ask for this specifically. If you would like to pre-order the food beforehand so the staff do not have to keep interrupting you, ask for this. There are many accommodations that can and should be made so everyone can have an enjoyable experience.

Before you go, write a small Social Story with your child. This doesn't have to be anything fancy – just a few stick pictures of what is going to happen. You can even get Social Stories from the internet for different events if you are unsure of your drawing skills! Show your child the pictures of the restaurant from the internet and explain to them in an age- and stage-appropriate manner what is going to happen when you get there, when you eat and when you are leaving. Preparation is absolutely key, for you and your child.

When we talk about preparation, I bet you know what is going to come next. The bag. Pack a bag with everything you can think of that will entertain your child – fidget toys, iPad, headphones, ear defenders, paper, pencils, toys, teddies, whatever you think your child may at some point play with for 30 seconds. Older children tend to be more easily impressed with a Switch console or phone, but younger children may need a variety of objects to keep them entertained and may end up playing with the cutlery on the table or the salt and pepper shakers!

In addition to all your entertainment equipment, don't be afraid to pack food for your child. If you would like to enjoy a meal with friends or family but you know your child is only going to eat their particular foods, explain this to the restaurant. The majority of the time, if this is explained in advance of your visit or on arrival, the staff are more than happy for your child to sit and eat their very own safe snacks while the rest of you enjoy your restaurant food.

Once you have been to the same restaurant a couple of times, your child may start to become familiar with it and feel more comfortable with their surroundings. This can help make it an easier outing. But don't worry if this doesn't happen. Sometimes, eating out is just too hard, and it may be that you need to wait until your child is more accepting to be able to eat out with them. Enjoying food together should be a pleasurable experience, and if it is going to cause stress for your child, and stress for you, then the timing may not be right.

On a final note, when you do go out, have an escape plan. If your child is feeling overwhelmed or goes into fight or flight, you may need a way to get out of the situation as quickly as possible. Plan for this in advance, be aware of how close you can park and what the quickest way home is. There might be a space you could go to locally that could calm them in the meantime. Sometimes entertainment venues have 'changing spaces' (bathrooms); it's useful to know where these are if you need a safe, enclosed room that is clean and away from all the noise of the outside world, where you can take your child until they can re-regulate. You can arrange with the restaurant to pay your bill upon ordering, so that if you do need to make a quick escape, you know your food bill is taken care of, or if you are pre-ordering your food before you go, you could even pay then to take the pressure off during the visit.

At the end of it all, if you can manage a meal out, enjoy it. Make happy memories without the pressure of it being the perfect meal. If you cannot yet manage it, that's okay; work up to it or enjoy lots of home-cooked meals and takeouts in your own home. Do what works for you and your family.

As a parent of a child with different needs, you are going to find that you have to do some things differently. You may have to go out of your way to do typical family activities, you may have to take a bag of toys or a bag of snacks, and you may not be able to get out as often as you'd like. But you will do what works for your family. Unfortunately, a lot of people are going to have opinions on your parenting. There are going to be people who look at you in a restaurant, while your child sits on their iPad and eats rice cakes, and they will judge you...they will *really* judge you. There are going to be people in your life, even in your family, who think you are 'giving in' to your child by allowing them to have their safe food. There are going to be school mums and teachers who judge you for the packed lunches you send. Unfortunately, not only is this a part of neurodiverse parenting, but it is a part of parenting in general. We keep coming back to the fact that you have to be your child's biggest advocate. You need to be the strong one, unapologetically, metaphorically and literally, shouting from the rooftops about what support your child needs. You will need to develop a thick skin to wash away those dirty looks and judging eyes. You can do this; you can be steadfast in your support and unwavering and relentless in advocating for your child. You've got this!

Food and health

Finally, we are going to touch on some medical and diagnostic elements of poor eating. As I am not a medical doctor or dietician, I am only going to give you an overview of some of the links between food and medical conditions. If you are concerned that your child is becoming unwell because of the lack of variety in their diet, it is really important you get in touch with a medical care provider (GP or paediatrician) and they can refer you to support services such as a dietician or a feeding and swallowing specialist within speech and language therapy. This advice is not meant as anything other than a brief understanding of the related conditions and it is not medical advice.

A lot of what we have talked about in relation to food fits into a diagnosis of avoidant and restrictive food intake disorder (ARFID). ARFID is a new term; it has only been in the American handbook for diagnosing (DSM-5) since 2013 and it was only introduced to the World Health Organization's ICD-11, which is used in the UK, in 2022. There is therefore not a huge amount known about it by medical professionals, and it is extremely difficult to get a formal diagnosis of ARFID. However, some areas are now taking on the new diagnostic criteria and even setting up ARFID clinics, so there is some change happening and it's always worth asking if there is a clinic in your local area. If you hear ARFID being spoken about in relation to your child, it is simply a way to describe their difficulties with food and how their difficulties present. These food challenges can be found in conjunction with many other diagnoses, such as autism spectrum disorder, ADHD, sensory processing disorder, or even just on its own as a single difficulty without other neurodiverse conditions involved.

It's important to be aware if your child does have food

aversions or even an ARFID-type eating disorder. Their lack of food intake, although difficult to manage, can lead to deficiencies in vital nutrients. The lack of a well-rounded diet can mean our children do not eat enough of the right foods and therefore can have additional issues of anaemia (low iron), calcium deficiencies, B-12 deficiencies, iodine deficiencies and more. It's really important to try to encourage your child to take a multivitamin to help balance out these issues. You can find multivitamins in many forms, including liquid (from experience, this does not taste very good!), tablets, chewy sweets and powder to go into liquids. A dietician can help you manage your child's needs for their vitamin intake and help you get the right types of support in place to make sure your child doesn't become unwell from their eating challenges.

Chapter 5

Downtime

The importance of downtime and play

What do I mean when I talk about downtime? I'm talking about that enjoyable, happy, relaxing time when your wonderful off-spring drift off into their bedrooms and play nicely for hours on end...oh, wait, no that doesn't happen to me either. However, I am talking about the times your children are either at home or at an organised activity that they enjoy and participate in voluntarily without being pressured or talked into it (for the most part!). All of our children, both neurotypical and neurodiverse, need their downtime, just as much as adults, if not more so. Evolutionarily speaking, a child's playtime is when they process the things they have learned in the world and make sense of them in their own minds. The 'play' that we observe of cars and trucks, playing house or small world play are often replications of things children have seen in their own lives. Play is also vital for children to practise their skills, both physically (block building, malleable play, mark making) and socially (turn taking, sharing, co-producing). Play helps us understand how things work and develops our critical thinking skills. We learn that bigger things can hold smaller things. We learn that when we throw something in a trajectory, it will fly across the room (my youngest's *favour-ite* pastime!). We learn that if we mix two different colours of playdough, they will inevitably turn into a brown-mush colour! The benefits of having unstructured free play, or downtime, have been evidenced within educational literature for a long time. This play is not only vital when we are younger; as our children grow, they need their own time to help them figure out this confusing world we live in and understand how they fit in it themselves.

You may be thinking, 'Well, my child is older than playdough and cars; this doesn't apply to them.' But believe me, these periods of downtime are needed right throughout childhood and adolescence. We even need downtime and 'playtime' as adults. We all need to decompress, be social, do something enjoyable; it is part of being human. These basic needs do not change because a child (or adult) has a different neurotype or way of thinking. Some children may find it harder or more confusing to process their world – but all the more reason to support them in exploring their downtime, allowing them the safe space to explore their knowledge and understanding. As children grow into teens, the social demands of life can become increasingly difficult and, particularly for girls, managing friendships and relationships can increase in difficulty. This is particularly the case where a child does not have a diagnosis, and this is the first time you may be noticing their difficulties. It is well documented that females present differently to males in neurodiverse conditions such as ASD and ADHD, and they often learn to camouflage their difficulties through their early years. Once the social and academic demands become too much, their ability to conceal their difficulties becomes more challenging and their neurodiverse traits become more apparent. Being aware of this can help you understand your child's need for relaxation time that you may not feel is productive. However, having studied and worked with children for my whole career, I can honestly reassure you that you do not need to have every minute of your child's day planned out with fruitful activities of museums and cake baking. It is perfectly okay – and actually beneficial – to allow them the freedom to explore their imaginations and even – wait for it – to be bored.

This chapter is going to discuss some of the most common downtime activities throughout childhood, although you may have more of your own to add! I will also try to help you understand how you can make the best of these activities to meet your child's needs and the mechanisms behind these needs. As I have done throughout the book, I will be discussing everything in broad terms of neurodiversity in children – this may be a diagnosed condition, but also may not be. You may feel your child has a different way of thinking, but you haven't yet received a diagnosis or aren't going to. The advice I provide here applies to any child that you feel may benefit from it. Your child does not have to have a diagnosis for you to benefit from being aware of their needs and accommodating their personality and way of thinking. The chapter will discuss the different activities based on ages and stages to make things easier for you to find; feel free to skip to the part that relates to your child! I will end the chapter talking about digital media in general as this is something that I specifically research and applies to all age groups.

Early years (0–5 years old)

In the early years, it's easy to think all children are doing is mindless playing. But children of this age are learning such valuable lessons. Over the past decade, changes to curriculums across the world have acknowledged the benefit of play in the early years by incorporating 'play-based learning' into their core delivery, allowing children in the early years and sometimes beyond to experience their learning through an engaging and interactive curriculum. The benefit of this for children is that they are learning all the time, whenever they are doing an activity that would be considered 'downtime' in any other age group.

When children are very young, below 18 months, it would be difficult to know if they have a different way of thinking or engaging, and therefore their downtime will look much like that of most children. However, from around 18 months old, many children begin to display some evidence that their way of thinking might be neurodiverse. Some of the ways this becomes apparent could be the means by which they relax and play.

One way in which young children enjoy using their bodies is to use their hands to create stimulus in front of their own eyes. Young infants may flick or flap their hands in front of their eyes or near their face. This is called a 'stim' or 'self-stimulatory behaviour' and it is completely harmless and fun for them. Your child may be craving some visual stimulation (have a look in Chapter 1 for our discussion about the sensory systems) and has found a way to provide this for themselves (aren't they clever!). In a similar way, your young child may play with their voice – this is also done by neurotypical infants but may present a little differently in a neurodiverse child.

When our youngest son was a baby, he didn't really babble or talk to us, but he did use his voice to make a deep croaking and gargling sound. He did this so often and for such a long period of time that we ended up getting him checked by an ear, nose and throat specialist who confirmed there was absolutely nothing wrong with his vocal cords – he just enjoyed making that sound.

As babies grow into toddlers, their play expands and their ability to use toys and equipment develops. Yet it is how they use these objects that can give clues as to whether they have a neurodiverse way of thinking. Your child may seem obsessive about a particular toy or soft object – this is common in very early childhood, and the object is referred to as a transitional object. However, if this attachment is particularly strong and continues beyond the early years, this may signify that they are using their transitional object as more than just a comforter and, in fact, need to have it in their presence to feel safe. When we talk about a transitional object, this is often a soft toy (for my son, it is his monkey), but there is no hard and fast rule. I have worked with children who carry around a toy, a dolly, a particular cup and even one of their dad's ties.

A transitional object is any object that your child is attached to emotionally. The object will provide comfort when they are upset and make them feel more secure in themselves. We call it a transitional object because the object moves with them – where they go, the object goes, and it is always there to provide this comfort when the child is upset, no matter where they are. For young children, this is really common, and a soft toy will often follow them to nursery or to Grandma's. However, as your child moves beyond this age bracket, if you find they are still clinging on to Dad's T-shirt or a particular Tupperware box of rocks that has to go with them everywhere, you may be dealing with a little more than you were expecting. If this is the case, it's okay: your child may be feeling insecure, anxious or just that they need a little bit more comfort. Try to get your child's nursery or school to accept your child bringing their transitional object into the setting. See if they can make arrangements for the object to be somewhere close by and within view; often this is all that is necessary to make the child feel secure. They should be allowed to access it when they need to, and it should never be taken away as a punishment from your child.

Imagine a transitional object as holding all the love and protection you feel for your child. Your child will begin to learn that they cannot have you around all the time, and this is where they will develop their relationship with a tangible object – something they know they can transport. For them, this object provides love, care, safety, comfort and confidence – every positive feeling you would wish to give your child during a difficult moment in their day when you cannot be with them.

Therefore, this object should be treated with absolute respect. This is the most important thing in your child's world, and that needs to be recognised. You can talk about the object and make your child aware that you understand how important it is to them. The object should only ever be used as something for comfort, as a cuddle would. It is never appropriate to use their source of emotional stability as a punishment for poor choices in behaviour. If you do this, you run the risk of alienating your child and teaching them that their emotional needs are not going to be met.

So what play could be considered downtime for a child in the early years age group?

Young children like to play with all sorts of objects, not just toys. You may find that your child takes an interest in a particular type of toy – bricks, cars, puzzles, etc. – or they may find themselves drawn towards non-play items – keys, remote controls, phones, etc. This can be true of both neurotypical and neurodiverse children, although you can find children with neurodiverse tendencies have a predisposition to enjoy non-traditional play objects. As long as this is safe (e.g. batteries removed), let them go for it!

Throughout raising all my children, we have made use of non-traditional objects to play with. Children are often fascinated with the objects they see adults use. You can make amazing sensory baskets of objects from things you find in the pound/dollar store. A bath scrunchie, an exfoliating glove, rubber mats, cork placemats, a door stop, a metal chain, wooden spoons. All these items are mundane and boring generally, but they can create hours of quiet exploration for a young child, and they have often found their way into our sensory baskets at home. Add in some fabrics – we have asked local material stalls for offcuts of different materials they have left over. These will allow your child safe exploration of different textiles and sensory inputs. Don't be afraid to explore and get creative – we have refilled drinks bottles with a mixture of water, oil and paint to create lava lamps (for your carpet's sake, please make sure you tape up the lids securely!). We have also repurposed baby milk tins and filled them with different objects (sticks, buttons, coins, etc.) to make shakers.

Then, of course, there are the objects that the children

see us play with – old mobile phones, remote controls you no longer use. We even have a wireless keyboard and mouse. During the pandemic of 2020 when I was working from home, my one-year-old would sit and type on his little keyboard because he saw Mummy doing it. Not all play items have to be bright colours and marketed specifically to children – sometimes the best afternoon's play is getting the pans and spoons out or creating a fort out of boxes!

All young children develop certain schemas within their play. That is to say, they develop specific ways they prefer to play and ways in which they use play to navigate their world. To adults, these ways of 'play' may not actually look like play – they may appear to be mischievousness or not listening. However, if you step into your child's world, you can get a better understanding of why they are playing in certain ways.

The following table describes the observable schemas in young children's play, together with some examples of what these may look like in day-to-day play.

Schema types and meanings

Schema	Meaning	Example
Trajectory	Movement in space.	Using their body or objects to see how they move in the space around them. Climbing on things, jumping off furniture and throwing toys are often seen within a trajectory schema.

Positioning	Putting toys or items into lines or groups.	A fan favourite is lining up cars or bricks, putting sweets into assorted colours, or similar.
Enveloping	Covering their own body or objects with other items. This includes placing the items into other containers or wrapping them up.	Placing smaller cars inside larger cars or trucks. Wrapping themselves up in blankets and playing underneath the blanket.
Rotating	Spinning themselves or objects.	Running around in circles, spinning on the spot, spinning the wheels on cars.
Enclosing	Keeping themselves or objects within specific physical boundaries.	Adding walls around their play using sofa cushions, enjoying playing within tents, adding borders to pictures, putting bricks (or similar) in walls around toys they are playing with.
Transporting	Moving items from one place to another or carrying toys with them.	Taking the toys from the table to the shelf to play. Adding toys into a bag and carrying them around with them.
Connecting	Putting things together and taking them apart again.	Building bricks, adding track pieces, sticking things with tape and glue.
Transforming	Transforming states of materials.	Mixing things such as sand and water. Watching how they move from one state to another.

cont.

Schema	Meaning	Example
Orienteering	Moving their body or objects into different positions.	Hanging upside down off things, moving things from one place to another or into different positions – upside down, sideways, etc.

Keeping these schemas in mind while giving your child a chance to have their downtime can make the experience more restful and enjoyable for you both. Looking at the schema of rotation, we often see this as a schema that does not progress into more significant play as a neurodiverse child gets older (that is not to say if your child does these things, it is a sign of neurodiversity – it is just one of many parts of your child that may make up a neurodiverse profile). Children with a rotation schema will often flip toy cars over (or even their own pushchair) to sit and spin the wheels. They may sit fascinated for hours on end watching the wheels go round and round. To an adult, this may be seen as 'naughty behaviour' (flipping the toys or pushchair over), but it's really just your child trying to discover their world and gain some enjoyment and exploration of their surroundings. So if you can safely allow them to flip the pushchair and spin the wheels, and they enjoy doing this, then why not allow it?

Similarly, other schemas can come under fire if misunderstood. Many of these schemas involve your child moving themselves and their bodies in new ways and exploring what they can do. Climbing and jumping (orienteering schema) and throwing things across the room and jumping off things (trajectory schema) come to mind. Often, when a three-year-old climbs the sofa and jumps off it, you would expect the parent or carer to react negatively – and maybe rightly so. Children still need to learn rules, boundaries and respect. However, from a schema standpoint, they are trying to develop their understanding of their world and how their body fits in and moves within it. Recognising this as a schema could help you work together with your little one to develop safe ways to use their play schemas. Find safe and constructive ways in which they can climb, and provide items to throw that are soft and safe.

Our youngest son currently has many schemas. He loves to line up his cars; he takes them out of the car tub and insists on lining them along the furniture – the floor is apparently not good enough! He enjoys putting all his smaller cars into his larger vehicles – in lines, of course – and closing them in there. Yet his favourite schema at the moment is his trajectory schema. He likes throwing things – a lot. All the knowledge of schemas in the world didn't stop me from crying into my hands a month before Christmas 2021, when he threw (a very good overarm throw) a small metal car at our main television, smashing it into 1001 sad little pieces – along with my sanity and bank balance. Sometimes, we can understand why our children are doing something and yet still be really unhappy about it. My husband and I have both had cars, remote controls, dummies and bottles thrown at us repeatedly – honestly, the child's aim is so good he always manages to hit our faces full on! All this is to say that I hope this information about schemas helps you understand your child and provide activities for them that allow them relaxation and downtime safely, but I also recognise that having this information doesn't always make it okay and it definitely doesn't always make it easier.

Childhood (5–12 years old)

As young children grow and develop, their skills will develop further and their play will change. Their interests may become more specific, as is common in many neurodiverse profiles. They may develop keen interests in one or two very specific things, and all their play and downtime may revolve around those. These interests might not make any sense to you, but they can mean everything in the world to your child. Whether this is a deep knowledge of every planet and star in the solar system, naming every dinosaur in each era or knowing everything about a particular pop group, your child may find themselves in a deep dive of information beyond what you would expect for their age. For neurodiverse boys, these are often clear to see as almost 'obsessions' with a specific subject. However, neurodiverse girls present very differently to boys; they often have more subtle idiosyncrasies which can often be overlooked as simply being 'girly'. Common interests in neurodiverse girls can be horses and ponies, clothes and make-up, and other such topics that would often be passed off as typical interests in girls. The difference, however, lies in how intensive and restrictive the focus your child puts on these topics. Nevertheless, you may find this is how they spend a lot of their time now they are older and more capable of exploring their interests through books and even digital media.

As children get older, the pressures placed on them also develop. By the time they are within this age range, they will most likely be entering into formal education on weekdays. Therefore, their downtime after school on these days and at weekends is vitally important in its restorative value. It is no longer just play for play's sake. Their time is now about both enjoyment and recovering from their week. As we have discussed in previous chapters, there are huge sensory demands throughout the day on many children with neurodiversities. Often, once home and in a safe place, many of those emotions and feelings will come out and manifest as emotional behaviours. Supporting your child during their downtime doesn't have to mean you constantly play with them or even provide them with activities. Often, it's about providing a safe comfortable retreat area within the home for them to relax in after school. This can give them a space to go where they will not be disturbed and they can spend some time re-regulating before rejoining activities with you or their siblings. This is what I call 'sensory downtime', and it can be a valuable tool in transitioning from one activity to the next. There is a certain sense of self-advocacy for your child to be able to relax and be alone to calm their senses; it can be incredibly empowering for your child to manage their own emotions.

Adolescence (13–18 years old)

Of course, as toddlers grow into children and children into teens, their need for relaxation and downtime will change. Adolescents have many social situations to deal with, and they may need more space and time out of these situations to calm themselves down and self-regulate. It is also very common at this age for children to pull away from their parental or carer figures and want to be more independent and assert themselves. This is really hard as a parent, when you want to know how your child is and if they are coping, but it's a perfectly natural part of growing up and important for them to begin to understand who they are without you for the time when they will go out into the world.

During this adolescent period, they may also want to spend time out with friends and go exploring more places. This can be tricky enough when your child is neurotypical, but when you have additional issues to be concerned about, it can put a lot of pressure on you to make the right decisions. Depending on your child's needs, they may be able to go out with friends – with the right support. Often, clear boundaries are vital to ensure your child knows what is expected of them and what they are and are not allowed to do. This includes physical boundaries of places they cannot go and areas you expect them to stay within. Neurodiverse children can often misinterpret information if it is vague; being precise about where you expect your child to be and at what times is essential in creating a trusting relationship. As well as physical boundaries, make sure your child knows what behaviour boundaries are expected of them when they go out – what kind of behaviour will be tolerated when they are with their friends (we all know children like to mess around when they are together) and what kind of behaviour is taking it too far (we also know they can get carried away). Having these conversations with your teenager before they go out allows them to know explicitly what is and isn't acceptable behaviour when they are out of your care and prevents miscommunication or false assumptions.

If your child isn't yet wanting to go out with friends or isn't at a developmental stage where this is an appropriate activity, allow them space at home to be themselves, however that may be. Your child is exploring who they are as an individual in the world. That might not be the same person you thought of when they were young, and it might not be who you expected them to be, but they are themselves. Allowing them to explore their interests and talents while relaxing gives them the freedom and safe space to know they are accepted.

I have one teenager who would spend every waking minute

straightening her hair and reapplying her make-up...and I have another teenager who would lie in bed for 12 hours reading book after book or drawing anime pictures. When it is downtime in our home, they are allowed to do what they want to do. If that means not leaving bed on a Sunday afternoon and finishing the latest novel, then so be it!

When thinking about neurodiverse teenagers specifically, it's worth noting that the world can feel extremely exhausting a lot of the time. Teenagers naturally have different sleep cycles to adults; they fall asleep later and wake later – it's biological. But they may also need extra time to sleep and rest to physically recover from making it through the day at school; this is really common. So if your child (like mine) comes home from school, crawls into bed and has an hour-long nap before they can function at home, allow them to do this. Providing you don't think they have some type of clinical depression causing excessive sleep, it is most likely they are burnt out from masking and camouflaging throughout the day, and their brain and their body need to catch up and reset.

When downtime doesn't feel relaxing

Depending on where your child's difficulties lie, they may find having downtime difficult for many reasons. Sometimes children can be overwhelmed with all the choices of what they can do, and not know how to spend their time. With some children, this can spark the most amazing creativity and resourcefulness – cardboard boxes that are spaceships, imaginative play in a far-off land and other unimaginable adventures (at least to our boring grown-up minds!). But to other children, this void of structured play can cause panic, even anxiety. The worry of doing something can be so paralysing that downtime can become a chore rather than an enjoyable experience. It can also be the case that a child can feel overwhelmed with such a huge number of thoughts and ideas that they do not know what they want to do – and therefore don't actually get to do anything in their downtime.

Both my eldest daughter and my eldest son struggle with 'there's-nothing-to-do-itis'. It's a common complaint in children. There can be a wide selection of entertainment on offer yet a severe lack of wanting to interact with anything offered to them.

Me: What would you like to do?

My child (pick a child – any child!): Shrugs shoulders.

Me: What about painting/baking/playing out/going for a walk/(insert any activity here)?

My child: Shrugs shoulders.

Me: What about watching a film together? Or playing your game?

My child: Shrugs shoulders.

Me: Well, what would *you* like to do?

My child: Dunno.

Me: (stares blankly)

My child: There's nothing to dooooo!

As frustrating as this is, it is actually difficult for neurodiverse brains to make decisions. This is a common theme across many neurodiverse conditions from ADHD to dyslexia and more. One of the best strategies I have found for helping this is to find two suitable choices that you know your child likes (e.g. going for a walk or baking) and offer those. This cuts down the indecision and can help your child focus on one particular thing. However, if they really won't make a decision and they really cannot enjoy their downtime, there is absolutely no harm in a little boredom. It inspires creativity and imagination. If your child cannot decide what to do with their downtime, ensure you communicate the boundaries of time – 'We have one hour of playtime now' – and if they do not want to choose an activity, then allow them to not have an activity at that time – 'Once the hour is up, it is up even if you do not play with anything.' This allows your child the freedom to be bored, but also the understanding that if they choose an activity at the end of the hour, the hour will still be finishing – not starting when they have chosen! (Which, believe me, my children have tried to do time and time again, and usually late at night!)

Digital media

We have all heard the horror stories printed in the press: some evil person did some evil act and it's all because they played a computer game. Well, as a researcher into digital media, let me tell you: it's not true. You do not have to be scared of letting your children have access to digital media, as long as it is used in the right ways – and this is something we will discuss here.

Currently, the research shows there is as much benefit to digital media use as there could be harm.[5] The idea that it is going to make children violent is outdated, and it is more likely the case that they are able to get out their frustration in a virtual world so that they don't do it in the physical world. In addition, many computer games require concentration, attention and memory skills. Children need to develop their fine motor skills to touch tablets and phones, and to use joypads on game consoles. They develop their coordination through movement, their planning skills on games with strategies and their communication skills on multi-player games. These are just a few of the benefits of digital media.

We are living through the digital age, and digital literacy is not only a skill we need but a requirement to be a functional member of society. You cannot call a taxi without at least a mobile phone (gone are the days of phone boxes!), you cannot go shopping without passing a self-scanning till, and you even cannot get a McDonald's without a touch screen. Therefore, as much as some may push against it, digital literacy skills are vital skills for child development.

So, how can we incorporate digital media into our neurodiverse children's downtime, I hear you ask!

First, I think it's important to take note of the added benefits digital media has for children with neurodiversities.

Let's start with all the bright colours! That's right, those beautiful bright colours of games are themselves enticing to children who may be needing visual sensory input. From a young age, babies and children are drawn towards television screens. This isn't a new development; even before tablets were invented, we had toys that we would wind up and the little paper screen would go round and round in a loop (I think we had a Teletubbies one for our children!). Young children are drawn to the movements of the bright colours. There is science that goes into why Mickey Mouse is the colour he is and how to keep young children engaged and watching (obviously, this applies to other shows too; it's just that I've watched so many Mickey Mouse episodes I might cry!).

Digital media also provides children with predictable outcomes: they can watch stories play out repeatedly. In fact, how many of you are sitting reading this after watching *Frozen* on repeat for months? Or *Cars*? *Moana*? Wait! I know...*Encanto*! 'We Don't Talk About Bruno' was the theme tune of our house for three months straight...daily...hourly...every minute (I hope you can feel my despair through the page!). I know you're there with me. Having these shows on repeat is exhausting for us, but for our precious little bundles, watching them again and again provides reassurance. They don't have to be anxious about what is going to happen. There is no pressure on them to learn new names or new stories or even new relationships.

For children – and adults, in fact – this stability can be really comforting. Even as a neurodiverse adult, I do the same. I watch the same TV show every night before bed to get to sleep. I don't have to look at the screen; I don't even have to listen closely to the words – I know it so well by now. But there is no pressure on my mind to work hard, and at the end of a long work day, I need that. I also have what I call my 'duvet' show – *Gilmore Girls*. Any episode of this show gives me the same feeling as being wrapped in a blanket with a cup of tea and a bar of chocolate. Digital media can give us this feeling of being secure and comfortable.

As children grow older, the online world has many more facets to explore, one of these being the ability to communicate through digital media. As a parent, I know exactly what you are thinking – 'I don't want my child talking to people on the internet!' – and rightly so. But done in a safe way, for children who find it difficult to communicate and make friends in real-life situations, digital media can provide a method of interacting with peers that feels comfortable to them. I wonder how many of you reading this leave a phone call to ring out and then text the person – I know I do. Or avoid people in the street but are happy to write on their Facebook wall – I know I do. And how many of you feel more comfortable being social through digital media than you do in real life? Again, I know I do. Children are no different, particularly children who have difficulties in social communication. These difficulties don't mean that they don't want to be social; they just find it that little bit harder. Therefore, digital media can play a huge part in supporting and scaffolding their social skills to help them interact with other children.

My eldest son loves gaming. At the age of ten, he isn't allowed to add the chat features on the games, as, like many parents, we don't want him talking to random strangers on the internet. However, what he does do is call or facetime his friends while they are playing the same game, and they play and talk about the game and their strategies on the phone. Sometimes there are silences, but that's okay; sometimes they are shouting to move to a different part of the game or some such instruction, and that is also okay. The communication they have been able to use through digital media allows them to interact in a way they would find difficult if they were simply on a phone call together to talk without an activity to mediate it.

Outdoor play

Finally, I want to discuss the benefits of outdoor play for neurodiverse children. There is a wealth of research to show that neurodiverse children – specifically, autistic children – spend less time in outdoor environments and get less exercise.[6] Many of the reasons for this have to do with the social nature of a lot of outdoor and sporting activities. Yet the majority of research also shows the benefits that the outdoor environment can have for our children's health, wellbeing and even thinking abilities.[7]

However, encouraging our children to go outside and play is a huge challenge sometimes. Part of this is because the outside environment can be so unpredictable, from the changing weather to the different environments that can all be found outside. When you add in all the different people you might meet, or animals (my goodness, if my son sees a bug anywhere near us, we have to go home, no matter how much I explain that this is where bugs live!), it's easy to see why the outdoors could feel so overwhelming. However, the benefits of being outdoors are so great that it's important to help our neurodiverse children get out there and get some exercise.

If your child doesn't like playing team sports, there are other ways in which you could get out and have fun in nature. Bike rides are always a good option in our house – a solitary sport for which no communication is required. It does, of course, mean that you need a bike and a suitable space to ride it, which I'm aware is not something everyone has. In fact, we don't have space to do this at home, in a busy suburb; it is only when we visit the Lake District that our children go off out on their bikes and enjoy the great outdoors. Other activities, such as walks together, can be made into fun activities for children, such as 'going on a bear hunt' or 'exploring', and can provide children with both exposure to outdoor environments and a little exercise while outdoors.

But don't get me wrong, I know that sometimes you need to choose your battles – we all do. Sometimes a day in on the games system is what they need to feel safe and secure, and trying to get them to do anything else is just going to cause stress for them and stress for you that you don't need. It's all about balance and managing their wants with their needs to ensure they are getting their downtime in a variety of ways.

Disclaimer: Do as I say and not as I do. My child is glued to his screen for a significant portion of the day, and often it's one fight too far for me. For my sanity and his, I allow it. One day I will follow screentime guidelines – today is not that day.

Chapter 6

Days Out and Going to New Places

Picture us in the middle of a large zoo. Elephants to the left, monkeys on the right. And my child screaming like a banshee in the middle. I'm sure we have all been there. Planned a lovely day trip with the best of intentions and yet everything that could go wrong has gone wrong. On our trip to the zoo, it was a new zoo we hadn't been to before, we didn't know our way round, we didn't take a picnic in the hope we could find food there and we waited 45 minutes in a queue to get some cold chips! And quite rightly, the kids were fed up. But our son was more than fed up; he was overwhelmed and exhausted and he just couldn't hold in all his feelings anymore. This led to a meltdown and, all of a sudden, he legged it! So now picture it, one parent sits with the three remaining children while the other hot-foots it through a zoo they don't know, chasing after a child in complete meltdown and unable to catch him – because I'm now in my mid-30s and running for anything other than the ice cream man is out of the question. As you can imagine, our perfectly planned day trip to the zoo ended there and then. Once the absconder was caught and calmed down, we promptly left the zoo.

The problem with days out ending like this is that it leaves a bad taste in your mouth for the next trip. As a parent or carer, you are left anxious and worrying about what the next trip will bring, and our children are anxious about going somewhere new again, or somewhere busy (not necessarily new), and not being able to cope. The main aim of a family day out is to have fun as a family and create shared positive memories. So, when it doesn't turn out like that, with all the planning in the world, it's disheartening and can make you feel like you don't want to do it again.

But don't fret – there are things you can do to make days out and new experiences as positive as possible. And there are de-escalation techniques you can use when you are out and about to try to keep everything on an even keel.

First off, it is important to recognise how big a step it is for our neurodiverse children to even try going somewhere new. I don't know about you, but going to new places fills me with anxiety even now as a full-grown adult. They say humans are creatures of habit, and, on the whole, that's true. We like to stick to things we know. I go to the same restaurants – I joke, I don't get to go to restaurants! – but I go to the same play centres, the same petrol stations and the same supermarkets all the time. In fact, I will deliberately drive miles out of my way to go to a supermarket I know better, even if I'm on the wrong side of town. As an adult, I have a choice in doing this. I know that with my own neurodiversity, if I go to a supermarket where the aisles are all out of order or not what I am expecting, I will feel overwhelmed and I won't be able to remember anything on my list. The list in my head is written according to how the supermarket goes from one aisle to the next. Switching that up is just too uncomfortable for me, and therefore I avoid it.

However, our children are younger, and there are experiences they may want to have, yet they may still feel the same anxiety as I do when I step foot in a supermarket that doesn't start at the vegetable aisle. Allowing our children to have these shared positive experiences is often what we think about when we are becoming parents, eager in anticipation for the zoo trips, the farms and the play centres. It isn't fair to limit them based on their neurodiversity, so we must expand the ways in which we can support them to have these experiences safely and calmly.

So, what can we do? I'm going to break this down into a few sections. As with everything else in the book, use what works for you. Your family circumstances, your parenting and your children may all contribute different views on what works. It may be a case of trial and error to see what works and what doesn't, but hopefully, with some of these suggestions, you can get out there with your family and enjoy some positive memories (and not chase them through a zoo like an out-of-breath panda!).

Preparing for the trip

Once you have decided you would like to go on a day trip, there are several things you can do to prepare your child(ren) for the day. My first suggestion would be to avoid going on a day out on a whim. As adults, sometimes, a spontaneous day out can feel fun and exciting and bring a sense of freedom and adventure to our largely regimented lives. However, for children who feel they have little control over things anyway, a spontaneous day out can be filled with so much anxiety and dread that they do not get to enjoy it. So, plan ahead – even if it's just a couple of days. This will give you time to put steps in place to help manage your child's anxieties and prepare them (and you) for the day. Having said that, do realise that if you plan too far in advance, or do not put a time on it, you may end up being pestered for the rest of eternity.

I have promised my 15-year-old a trip out, just me and her, shopping at the local independent shops and then sushi for lunch. I made this promise with the absolute best of intentions, but we still haven't been. I'm sure many parents can relate to me here when I say that life just keeps getting in the way. With three other children to find childcare for, work and other commitments, there just hasn't been a day to go. Don't you worry, though, my daughter has not forgotten...and she will not forget. She may not remember to take the right equipment to school, she may not remember to put anything away, she may not remember to do her homework...but she *will* remember this. And she will remind me constantly until the date is set and we have gone.

A great way of preparing your child for the upcoming trip is using Social Stories or timelines. These don't have to be anything spectacular in design and can even just be hand-drawn scribbles. A drawn visual image of what you are going to be doing can be so beneficial. Give your child an indication of the day the trip will happen, whether in words or in another way. Give them an idea of what will happen on the day, how you will travel there and who will be going with them.

All these things will help your child develop a sense of control over what is going to happen during the trip. This control will ease them into the trip a little easier. (One of my favourite phrases is 'Knowledge is power' – in this case, it is absolutely true.) Another way of supporting your child to prepare for the trip is to show them images of the places you are going. Online searches are a great way to do this! Often your child's mind will be full of questions about what the place is like: is it going to be loud, is it going to be busy, what is it going to look like? All these uncertainties can make a trip, even an enjoyable trip, feel overwhelming. Therefore, looking at a few pictures online can take the mystery out of your trip and help your child feel more comfortable with going.

We often use online pictures to look at where we are going. My eldest son will come to me if he is feeling uncertain and he will ask to see what a place looks like. Last summer, we were going to a farm for a whole day out, and although excited, he was nervous. Particularly as I had talked about it having a 'Maize Maze'. Well, of course, he had absolutely no idea what this was, and I had absolutely no idea that he didn't know. Cue a lot of confusion! So we went online, and we looked through all the pictures the farm had on their website, then on their social media pages and then on TripAdvisor (this boy likes a lot of information!). Having looked through all these pictures, we felt we knew this farm and all its facilities inside out. Yet the next day he comes to me again, and we look through all the pictures again (and let me tell you, you cannot get away with showing fewer pictures – they know, and they will call you out for this!). Again, the next day we looked again...you get the idea. Eventually, the day of the farm visit came, and my wonderful son was basically a tour guide for the rest of the family, proudly showing everyone around and letting them know what the farm had. The only place he couldn't get to show us around was the Maize Maze!

Another way to support your child in the run-up to a big event or trip out is using a calendar to count down the days. Again, this gives a tangible visual representation to your child to understand the context of time. For young children, a day, a few days and a week can all seem like an eternity. Therefore, having something to show them visually how long the wait is can be really useful.

Every school holiday, we get the whiteboard out. I use a marker and break down the board into how many days we have off school plus a day either side. On the first and last square, I place the word 'school', which helps my son understand that this time starts from the last day of school until we are due to go back to school. On the other days, I will place the activities we are doing. Some squares are rightfully empty – we cannot manage to do something every day! But when there is a big event like a trip out, that is written on the board. The children love to use this board to check what we are doing and count the days until something exciting is happening. For us, we often place on the board if the children are going to Grandma's one day, or if they are booked into holiday club. This way, it doesn't sneak up on them and they can be prepared for what changes may be coming.

Example whiteboard chart

Saturday	Sunday	Monday	Tuesday	Wednesday	Thursday	Friday
						School finishes
	Going to Grandma's for tea			Zoo trip!		Play centre
Trip to the park		Visiting the museum			Holiday club day	
		School starts				

The day before the trip, make sure you have gone over the plans with your child. For some children, once can be enough; others (like my son) may want you to repeat these plans again and again until your mouth is dry and you have no words left. Roll with it. They are just trying to get the plan in their heads to help them feel more comfortable, and, honestly, it's going to help you all have a more peaceful trip in the long run.

Use the day before to go over the timelines one final time. Look at the pictures and discuss the plan for the day, remembering to include travel arrangements and who is going. At this point, nothing should be a surprise for your child(ren). And tuck them into bed going over it again (trust me, this is unlikely to be a choice: they are going to pester you to death with excitement the night before!).

In terms of your own preparations the day before, as with everything else we have discussed, preparation is key. Pack the kids' bags with things they will enjoy, such as favourite toys, fidget items, a tablet device if they use one. These are the things that are going to make your journey easier. Whether you are travelling in a car or on public transport, each has its own difficulties when travelling with children, and you are going to need some tools at hand to get you through the journey! Similarly, you will also need to pack the essentials that your child needs, rather than wants. Nappies and wipes are always my favourite things to forget – so if your child is in nappies, pack hundreds. (Side note: I have forgotten nappies and wipes so many times I now have a dedicated bag full of nappies and wipes in the boot of my car because I will more than likely forget to pack them in the children's day bags and end up having to buy expensive ones from service stations!) Do they need specific food or particular snacks? Don't forget to put them in the bag. A change of clothes because, well, you know what kids are like! A sunhat if it gets sunny and, of course, a coat as well because of unpredictable weather. Have you packed their reins/harness if they use them? All these things need to be ready to go for the trip the night before, because I promise you, if it's left to the day, something will get left behind (hence the nappies-and-wipes car bag!).

It's trip day!

The day is here and the excitement is high! Or maybe not? Some children love days out and going to visit new places – other children, not so much. Try not to take it personally if you have planned this wonderful trip only for your child to be less than enthusiastic about it. To put it bluntly, it's not you, it's them. But that's okay. It's okay for them not to be overly enthused about a trip; hopefully, they will still enjoy it at the end of the day. (If, like me, you live with teens, you will soon get used to the less enthusiastic child, and if your child isn't a teen yet, you will learn soon!)

While getting ready on the morning of the trip, try to keep things as calm and relaxed as possible. Your child may already be anxious about going somewhere out of their routine and/or somewhere new. Even with the huge amount of prep you have put into supporting them in the run-up to today, that anxiety is going to be there. This anxiety can build up and be demonstrated in so many different ways. It could show itself as positive excitement – you know, the bouncing-around-the-house-and-furniture type where they ask 'Are we nearly there yet?' a million times. It could present itself as shy retiring nervousness; they are excited to go on the trip but they just can't get to the point of enjoying that excitement because of all the unknowns. Or it could come out as the absolute opposite: the angry, frustrated and built-up type of anxiety, where they say they don't want to go on the trip, and they hate everyone and everything around them (including you). No matter how your child is displaying their feelings on this morning, practise patience and kindness with them. There is a lot going on today, and being mindful of that will get you both a lot further than getting mad or frustrated with each other.

Before you leave, go over the plan again – once, twice, a hundred times if they feel they need it. Also, use your support strategies, whatever they may be (visual timetables, now-and-next boards, online pictures). Remind them where they are going, who is going, how they are getting there and what they are going to do. Reaffirm their sense of control over their day trip – remember, knowledge is power.

Now, you're on your way. Your destination may be local enough to walk to, or you may be driving, getting a hired car, a minibus, a bus, a train or even a plane. One thing I can almost guarantee you will be asked by the verbal children in your travelling party is – you guessed it – 'Are we nearly there yet?' It's the age-old question that every parent dreads. The thing to remember with neurodiverse children is that they may take what you say very literally. If they ask 'Are we nearly there?' and you tell them 'Yes, a few minutes', meaning 15–20 minutes or more, they are going to struggle with that kind of wait when their expectation is that they will be arriving in a very short time. Similarly, if they ask 'Are we nearly there?' and you keep replying 'Not far' or 'Nearly there', their expectations are going to be mismatched with the realities of the wait they may have. It is for this reason that I would try to be fully upfront with any children you are travelling with. Often a conversation explaining that the travel may take a long time and that you know this will be difficult for them, but you are proud of them for being patient, can be all it takes to make the difference between a journey full of moaning and one without.

We are lucky enough to be able to connect our car to our phones, which means we get to use the satnav on the phone. For us, this has been such a godsend. For every journey we do, even the mundane everyday journeys like the school run, we pop the address into the satnav and the screen will tell us exactly how many minutes it will take until we get to where we are going (I'm sure you're all aware how satnav works...). For us this means that our son, who sits in the back, can see minute by minute how long the journey is going to take and when we are going to be there. He knows that when we travel long distances, it is going to take a long time, and that's okay, because he doesn't feel tricked into thinking we're nearly there when we are not. He often uses this opportunity to direct us or give us a running commentary of how long it's going to take us. But he isn't asking 'Are we nearly there yet?' For those who don't drive, many phones have built-in navigational systems, and allowing your child to map out the journey or follow it in real time using your phone can be of huge benefit to you both.

Finally, you have arrived!

So, you have done all the prep, you have travelled the distance, you have arrived!

Arriving at a new place or somewhere you have gone for a day trip can be stressful, particularly with children, and when you add in neurodiverse children, that is a lot to contend with. You may be trying to queue up for tickets or get wristbands, or trying to navigate your way around a new environment. It's understandable for both adults and children to be overwhelmed on arrival.

There are several things you can do to mitigate the stress – and you have every right to ask for this support (diagnosis or not!).

Get your tickets in advance – lots of tickets can now be purchased online and over the phone. This means you can skip the queues to get in and avoid those delays when you arrive. I know for certain my children do not do well waiting in queues, even for a short time. Every time we can buy tickets in advance, we do.

When getting your tickets, see if there is a 'fast pass' available. Many venues provide fast passes if you can take proof of your child's additional needs. If you have this, then use it wherever you can to make life easier for you and your children. If you do not have a diagnosis yet, don't feel you cannot ask; sometimes just explaining your child's needs will be enough. However, in many cases you can also pay to have fast passes; we have done this before, and it is well worth the money spent. Skipping the queues with fast passes helps you get your little ones on to the rides or into the attractions first. This cuts down on their time waiting, their time needed to be patient, their ability to regulate and their sensory overload – giving you a longer time with your children to enjoy your day out without having to worry about them as much.

Similarly, if you are flying or travelling on trains, you can register for travel assistance (you do not need any diagnosis for this). Airports and train stations can provide you with assistance in getting through their venues with less hassle and stress. Often you can skip the queues at baggage check-in, security and boarding. As with the entertainment venues, this queue skipping, while making things incredibly convenient for you, also supports your children in having the most calm and relaxed process, thereby keeping them regulated. Registering for assistance can also mean that you have access to quieter areas to wait, and even a sensory room at some venues. Thankfully, an increasing number of business and travel companies are recognising the need to support those who may struggle with crowded, loud, busy venues.

Moving on from travel and into the venue, if they have maps, one thing we have learned over the years is to get several! Maps are a great way to help you as adults plan out your day; however, they are also great for your children to feel a sense of understanding about where they are in this new place. A map can give them the power to feel safe in their surroundings because it no longer feels new and strange; now it feels familiar and logical.

Recently, we went on a trip to a new place. We followed all the steps and all the good advice, and we got two maps when we got there, one for us and one for our son, thinking that our 15-year-old was too old to need a map. Well, of course, we were wrong, and there soon followed a frantic dash back for more maps so everyone could have one. I would like to say this was where our drama finished, but then it rained – extremely heavily – for hours. So then we had several very soggy maps, which were of no use to anyone, and we had to keep stopping at the big signposting maps. So just to reassure you, you can plan all you like, but sometimes it's just not going to work out – and that's okay!

When researching your trip beforehand on the internet, as well as accessing photos of the venue before you visit, you could also have a look to see if there are maps online. This gives you and your child a chance to be one step ahead of the game and take a peek before you even get there.

So now the time has come to cuddle your little cherubs up, tuck their tired bodies and sleepy heads into the car and drive home peacefully...oh, wait, no, sorry that's not right. Now is the time to argue with a mini army of humans that they must leave the place they have spent the day complaining about to go back home, to the other place they continuously argue and complain about. That's right, folks – it's home time.

As with everything else we have discussed, preparation is key. Whether you use a now-and-next ('We will go on this last ride, and then it's home time') or a countdown ('We have 20 minutes...15 minutes...ten minutes left in the zoo'), give them some warning of the change that is about to happen. Not only is it a change, which is difficult anyway, but it's also likely they have spent a significant amount of time acclimatising to their new surroundings to only now be told they are leaving them. Be patient. You may say it's home time and they may get very upset – this is perfectly understandable for children, neurodivergent or not. They are in a fun place, and now they are being told they can't enjoy that fun anymore. To them, there may still be a dozen different things they want to do that you just don't have time for on this visit. Manage these expectations by explaining when they might be able to return. Be realistic about this – don't promise another trip the next day or next week if this isn't something that you are going to be able to manage.

Furthermore, this reminder about the world outside of their little trip may trigger them to remember all the other things in life that are making them anxious. Suddenly, they may start thinking about the journey, worrying they are going to be uncomfortable, worrying about what happens when they get home – is it bath time, is it bedtime, when will they play, what happens tomorrow? This small change from one place to another can trigger a flow of worries and anxieties that you may never know about. Whether they are verbal or pre-verbal, remember that your child is unlikely to tell you these anxieties; they may not even realise they are thinking them. But this may show in their behaviour – anger, shouting, defiance and, for some, absconding (running away). Try to be as patient as possible with this wonderful child who is screaming and hitting you in public. I know it's difficult, and it doesn't help you at the time, but they honestly don't mean it. (Sorry, I know how patronising that is, and it really does not help you at all, but it is important to remember!)

On a recent play centre visit (which in itself was a terrible idea because I was on my own with three children and no back-up!), I gave the countdowns. I told them we were going soon, mainly because we had wristbands that only allowed us 90 minutes before we were kicked out. But, of course, my toddler doesn't really get countdowns just yet, and I hadn't brought picture cards, so we just had to try to converse in a strange English-to-toddler translation. When he did realise that we were getting our shoes on and leaving the super-fun play centre, he was not happy. So unhappy, in fact, that he decided to throw his shoe (and, boy, does he have a good throw!), and this lovely toddler shoe goes flying across to the next table hitting a lovely lady's cup of coffee and spilling it everywhere!

As you can see, there can be some bad reactions to leaving places. Unfortunately, by this point in the day, your children may be overtired, overstimulated and dysregulated, while, simultaneously, you are exhausted, wishing you hadn't even bothered and most likely bursting for the toilet because you haven't taken your eagle eyes off your children all day. At this point, do what you can to manage behaviours but, generally, just be understanding. Accept their feelings and try to get them back into a comfortable environment to re-regulate as quickly as possible.

After your trip is finished – maybe on the way home if any of you can manage it, or maybe a few days later – try to do a quick debrief with your child. You can do this in any way that is suitable for them – a conversation, pictures, a song or some other means. Try to cover what you did and saw; discuss things you found fun and even things you didn't like or were difficult. If your children are verbal, you could encourage them to do the same. This will be useful in two ways. First, it will help them consolidate their memories of the place you visited, helping them be more comfortable next time. Second, it will help them understand their feelings for the place they visited. They may have had a fantastic time, or they may have struggled but had some good moments. With your encouragement, they can learn that it is okay to not enjoy everything, and those feelings are valid. But it will also help them remember the good points so the bad feelings don't overwhelm them, making them anxious or afraid of visiting the venue the next time.

Finally, even with all the preparation, all the planning and all the managing of the behaviours of several tiny humans in a public space, try to enjoy it. Days out, trips, travelling, eating out...it can all be overwhelming for parents too, particularly parents of children with additional needs. It can often feel as though you are only there to facilitate the children having a calm and enjoyable experience. But try to remember these are your family memories too. We only get small children (or medium or large) for 18 years. And later into those years, I've found they want to spend less and less time with you going on trips to the zoo and the play centre. So try to treasure those memories – those imperfect days out, the arguing siblings, the whining and moaning, and hopefully the laughs and giggles too.

Chapter 7

Bedtime and Night-Time

Do you remember those weary nights when you had a newborn? They were up so much in the night, but you didn't really mind – you looked at their angelic face and remembered it was all worth it. Well, that feeling gets tiresome when they're ten and still haven't had a good night's sleep. I'm sure we are not the only ones who feel like this. I cannot stress enough how much I love my sleep; the best gift I could be given would be childcare for a few hours so I can go back to bed. Sleep is precious, and I cannot understand why these tiny (and not so tiny) humans don't want to spend more time asleep... Apparently, it's just not on their agenda (screams internally!).

In this chapter, I will talk you through some of the different ways sleep can be affected by a neurodiverse brain, because it is not just struggling to fall asleep that can be the issue. We will also discuss ways in which this can affect your child and the rest of the family. Finally, we will go on to look at ways in which you can support your child's sleep – and, in turn, get more sleep yourself!

Sleep issues in children

First, we need to consider how children's sleep is affected in different ways. Every person is different generally, and we all have different sleep cycles; add into this a neurodiverse brain and the sleep cycles can be significantly different.

The most obvious issue around sleep has to be difficulty in falling asleep. When we discuss sleep issues in neurodiverse children, this is often what many people think of. We have all experienced it – lying in bed willing ourselves to get to sleep, yet nothing happens. Typically, as we gear down for bed, our body recognises that the light is fading, recognises the social cues of getting pyjamas on and washing, and melatonin begins to be produced. However, research has shown that in autistic individuals, this melatonin is not produced, or at least not in the amount needed for restful sleep. Therefore, that 'sleepy' feeling neurotypical individuals get at the end of the day doesn't occur.[8] However, this is just one theory and doesn't account for many other neurodiverse children who struggle with sleep. In other neurodiversities such as ADHD, it is possible that the brain cannot calm down enough to allow the melatonin to be released; therefore, the melatonin theory still stands, albeit for different reasons. There is currently a significant amount of research examining the reasoning behind sleep difficulties in neurodiverse individuals, but no matter the reasoning behind it, what is important is that we can do something to help it.

In addition to not going to sleep or taking a long time to fall asleep, children can also have issues with night-time waking. They may go to sleep well, but then suddenly wake in the night and be unable to get back to sleep. There it is – 3 a.m. and they are wide awake and ready for the day (my youngest child's favourite trick). There is nothing worse than being lulled into the false sense of security that you are going to get a good night's sleep... and then being tricked out of it, literally at the eleventh hour!

When our youngest son was between the ages of 12 and 24 months, he would spend on average five hours a night wide awake. At the time, he was in a regular cot at the side of my bed and could climb out of it (as we found out when he did so and fell to the floor, resulting in an A&E trip – with a wonderfully understanding doctor, who realised I was more shaken up than the baby was!). So, night after night I would put him to bed, and try to get an early night, because I knew around midnight he would be up and awake for hours. In the most typically ironic fashion, he would always fall back to sleep just before the alarm went off to get up in the morning – meaning I wouldn't be able to go back to sleep. Those were some hard times.

Let us say, by some miracle, your child goes to sleep well and doesn't wake up wanting a midnight party most nights of the week (oh, lucky you!); one of the other ways children can have sleep issues is through 'night terrors'. Night terrors are similar to a nightmare but your child is still absolutely sound asleep. For a parent or carer, this can be extremely confusing, challenging and, in fact, quite upsetting. Night terrors can happen in both neurotypical children and neurodiverse children, but we know from research that sleep difficulties in general are more often found in neurodiverse children.[9] This isn't to say that if your child has one or more of these sleep issues, they are neurodiverse because of this, but if you are already thinking about neurodiversities and your child, and they have a sleep issue, then they may be linked.

Night terrors often occur in the first few hours of sleep and happen when your child is in the non-REM type of sleep (the lighter sleep). Your child may wake up screaming and crying and appear to be distinctly afraid of something. It is often the case that the child will seem awake – they will have their eyes open and appear to have woken up from a nightmare. The difference between a nightmare and a night terror is that after a nightmare your child may wake up and be able to remember the nightmare but will not still be experiencing it. They will be able to talk to you (if they are verbal) and they will be able to understand you. However, when you talk to a child having a night terror, it will appear as if they cannot hear you or aren't listening to you. They may not be comforted by you and will continue to be afraid of what they are experiencing.

Night terrors can be really frightening for a parent or carer to experience with a child – the first time our oldest son experienced one, we were terrified for him – but more often than not, after the child has gone back to sleep and woken the next morning, they have no recollection of it ever happening (phew!). It is purely within their dream state, and they don't continue that fear to the morning.

One final way we are going to discuss sleep being affected is hypersomnia. This is where a child feels they need to sleep too much. They can feel tired a lot, and they may go to sleep early and sleep later. This may not feel like a big issue, but when their sleep becomes something that is preventing them from having a full day's activities, or they are still tired during the day because you have had to disturb their sleep, it can become an issue. If your child really does like their sleep, there could be many reasons for this in addition to hypersomnia. Becoming overwhelmed by sensory input can make us tired, as can having to be sociable and mask a lot. Therefore, before putting oversleeping down to hypersomnia, it would be prudent to first try to work out if anything is causing your child to feel so tired.

When discussing sleep, we also need to remember that children and adolescents have different sleep cycles compared with adults. Young children need a lot more sleep (from 16 hours as babies, 14 hours as toddlers and 11 as school children). Once children reach adolescence, they still need around ten hours of sleep per night; however, their sleep rhythm (often known as circadian rhythm) changes and you may find they don't feel sleepy until later at night and will need to sleep in longer in the morning – something that is not suited to the Western education system. Nonetheless, knowing why your teen may not want to get out of bed (or even go to bed at night) is important in understanding life from their perspective (I remember – as I'm sure my mother does too – being the same at that age!).

Our teenagers are in this phase at the moment, but they forget that the internet gives them away. When I check their WhatsApp in the morning, and it tells me they were last online at 2 a.m., then they know they're in trouble!

Effects of poor sleep

The negative effects of poor sleep are well established. Everyone, neurotypical and neurodiverse, struggles when we're living off little sleep (do not talk to me before my morning coffee – I am not very good company!). However, for those with neurodiversities, having little sleep can cause further issues and increase any difficulties they may have. For example, poor sleep can increase stress, both psychologically and physically. It can decrease our cognitive functioning ability, which leads to poor memory, poor concentration, decreased sociability, decreased optimism and lowered creativity. Can you imagine sending your child to school after a poor night's sleep and them having to battle to concentrate, to think clearly, to remember what the teacher has asked of them – and then getting in trouble when they couldn't do it? As adults, many of us can rely on a cup of coffee or a similar source of caffeine to get us through a bad night's sleep. Our children don't have this same option. It's worth considering when they have had a bad day at school if lack of sleep could be a factor in that.

As well as cognitive struggles, lack of sleep can lead to increased blood pressure, increased appetite and food consumption, and increased risk of heart problems. These are mostly small risks in children, but it's worth noting that having a prolonged lack of sleep is going to have a physical effect on their little bodies (as well as your own!).

So, we can see that having a good amount of sleep is important not only for your child but also for you. We work best when we are well rested. And this goes for your children too...

Have you heard of the witching hour? That time between when your child gets tired and when they actually go to sleep. Where everything you do for them is wrong, every snack you bring them is wrong, everything you say to them is wrong... That, my friends, is tiredness. Do not go near the children at this time... Throw the snacks from a distance and save yourself.

The thing that strikes me when there is a child in the house who doesn't sleep well is that they make it very well known. Therefore, on the whole, the rest of the family doesn't get much sleep either. When this happens, everyone becomes tired, everyone becomes grumpy, and everyone has that short fuse that leads to snapping at each other (I am certain you know what I mean!).

So, now we move on to why your child may sleep poorly and how we can tackle that to help your child and the whole family get more sleep.

Reasons for poor sleep

There are many different theories about why neurodiverse children have poor sleep patterns; some of these are social theories and some are biological theories. In reality, it is likely to be a mix of both of these things that contribute to children having poor sleep.

Looking at sleep issues from a social perspective first, children with neurodiversities can have difficulties with change, and therefore changing from afternoon to evening can be a difficult transition. It can make it difficult for them to settle down for the night and move into a calmer mood from their daytime activities. In addition, neurodiverse children can have difficulties in understanding the cues for night-time and bedtime. This is known as 'social cueing'. In neurotypical individuals, cues such as it going dark outside, lamps going on, having an evening meal, having a bath may all signal to the body that it will soon be time for sleep. Humans rely on routines, and those routines serve the purpose of understanding what is about to happen next. However, it is theorised that these social cues are not subtly picked up in the minds of some neurodiverse children, and therefore their brains do not start preparing them for sleep. Typically, once our brain recognises these patterns in our behaviour, it will release a chemical needed for sleep called melatonin. Gradually, melatonin will increase, and we will feel tired enough to fall asleep.

This leads us nicely into the biological theories of sleep, such as the melatonin theory. This theory suggests that neurodiverse individuals do not produce as much melatonin to trigger their brains to sleep, and therefore they can spend much of the night unable to sleep. This is something that has been supported by research over the past couple of decades.[10] It's unclear if this is because of social cueing or because of a biological irregularity. Nonetheless, decreased melatonin explains the difficulties many neurodiverse individuals have with their sleep.

This can be further exacerbated by natural changes in the sleep–wake cycle of individuals with neurodiversities. As we discussed earlier, children and adolescents often have different sleep cycles to adults naturally. Adding in the issues around social cueing and under-production of melatonin, you can understand why their natural sleep–wake cycle may be different from that of a neurotypical individual.

Building on this, we know from previous chapters that children with neurodiversities also have difficulties with sensory issues. These do not stop because it is night-time. The sheets may feel too scratchy, the pillow may be too soft, the room may feel too cold or too hot – any number of things may be triggering their sensory system. This may be difficult because your child may not be able to pinpoint what the issue is or even communicate it to you. Trying to get their perfect bedtime environment can be a huge challenge in itself.

Finally, the one thing that can be universal in keeping us up at night – our dear friend, anxiety. Children often worry and ruminate on their worries at bedtime. This is likely the first time in the day when they have had a moment of stillness and time not focused on other activities, and therefore it can often be a time for all those worries and anxieties to come to the forefront of their mind (I don't know about you, but this is exactly what happens to me too!).

It's not surprising really that, with all this going on, our neurodiverse children are having such a difficult time sleeping! So, let's take a look at what we can do to help them (and you) get that good night's sleep.

Ways to help with sleep

Routine, routine, routine...

We have all heard about the importance of routine for children and we have discussed its importance throughout the book for children with neurodiversities. However, it's important to continue this routine into the evening and to bedtime. As adults, we tend to have our own rituals and routines before bedtime: locking up the house, our skincare routine or just which side of the bed we sleep on. We keep coming back to the idea that humans are creatures of habit. These habits and rituals are often significant to us personally and help us make order of our lives. Therefore, it is so important to continue routine into bedtime for neurodiverse children. Often, neurodiverse children may struggle to recognise social cues that bedtime may be close, so making it clear that bedtime is about to begin will help your child prepare mentally for it. This routine also allows a buffer of time between knowing bedtime is coming and bedtime happening. Having this can be vital in ensuring your child has time to process the change in activity. Bedtime routines do not have to be anything extravagant, as long as they are consistent; keep doing the same thing, day in and day out. It will soon become a recognisable routine.

In our home, we have different routines for different children. With such a wide variety of ages in the house, we recognise they all need different things at different times. For now, I'll discuss the youngest. We start with a bedtime yoghurt. When he's eating this, we talk about what we're going to do next (go up to bed), and we talk about it being late and nearly bedtime – but not bedtime yet. He then gets ten minutes to sit and relax and watch a cartoon before we go upstairs. Once we're upstairs, we go to the bedroom and get pyjamas on, and often we will talk about what we are doing tomorrow (or after wake-up time, in his words). We then get on to his bed, and he is allowed to choose two books from the shelf, which we sit together and read. After this, he gets tucked in and kissed, and he knows it's bedtime.

It sounds angelic, doesn't it? Don't be fooled into thinking it's easy. A routine may help, but it does not change a three-year-old from not wanting to go to bed. When I tell you he gets pyjamas on...he is usually bouncing around the bed. When he is reading stories...he usually wants a third, fourth and fifth story. And when I say he gets tucked in...he will be climbing back out within minutes. However, all of this would be much more extreme behaviour had we not put routines into place. He knows that when it is time for yoghurt, it is nearly bedtime. Additionally, he often knows what comes next in the routine. Having this knowledge is empowering for our children; in a world where everything can feel big and confusing, it gives them some control and stability.

For older children, routines can look a little different. It is not as easy to tuck in a ten-year-old, and try tucking in a 15-year-old and you will get a mouthful. Therefore, it's important to recognise what a routine looks like for you and your children.

For our ten-year-old son, we allow him his evenings to relax, rebalance and do the things he enjoys. This is good for his overall health and wellbeing and allows him to recover from the stresses he deals with each day at school and in his relationships. But it makes things difficult for us when we need him to stop the activities he enjoys and go to bed. At this age, we have found giving a countdown timer works well; used consistently, it is respected. We let him know significant points before bedtime – one hour, 30 minutes, 15 minutes, ten minutes and finally five minutes. When these timers are done, it's bathroom time, a snack and a drink, and then into bed. Often, he tells us he is not tired and cannot sleep. In response, we just ask him to lie down and rest his body in the hope that doing this long enough will allow sleep to come – it often doesn't, though. As with our youngest, none of these recommendations is a quick and easy hack to get your children to sleep – they most likely won't sleep (because small humans like to make us suffer and live off coffee). However, they might make a difference in how well they initially settle, and doing this again and again, day in, day out, will provide your child with a pathway to better sleep.

As you can see, our children do very different things

before bedtime. This extends to our teenagers. One thing we notice with the oldest child is the difficulty she has in slowing down and relaxing before bed. This child is more like me than I often care to admit. She is brilliant, talented, full of ideas and thoughts which come at the most inconvenient times. She struggles to allow her body to rest before bedtime and can often find herself in an overstimulated, fight-or-flight response late at night. For us, the priority with our teenage children is respecting the fact that they have different sleep patterns but still need to get enough sleep and rest. This often consists of encouraging them to spend time relaxing, watching TV or playing a game rather than starting a new project at midnight. Reminders throughout the evening to not forget to chill can be beneficial to trigger some calmer time – although we are not always listened to!

This mixture of different approaches works for us (for now), and what works for you and your family may be different. The main point to take away is the benefit of the same routine each night – the same timings, the same methods and the same consistency. I would note, though, that we are aware that sometimes a little leeway is required for the children (and your own sanity). For example, if we had done an hour's worth of countdown to bedtime and then my son declared there were still four minutes left on his video, we would not make him switch it off at that point just because the timer says so. Making him turn it off at that point would cause a bigger reaction and a more difficult bedtime than making it clear that the end of the video is when bedtime will begin. As I tell my friends often, as parents we must pick our battles! Those four minutes will not significantly affect the amount of sleep he gets, whereas not letting him finish his video will disrupt his night and our night (and likely the other children) in a significant way.

Therefore, it seems pertinent to summarise this as *routine is important, but rigid routine is not.*

There are some wind-down activities that can be incorporated into the bedtime routine to help the transition into bedtime. There are some tried and tested methods that can aid sleep. Some of these may work, some may not, but everything is worth a try!

Bath time

Encouraging bath time before bed and in the bedtime routine can help your child's body to relax and calm before sleep time. It can give them some relaxation from their day and help them physically calm down. Of course, some children love baths and water – and some hate them. If bath time is going to trigger stress and anxiety, then do not try to include it every night; the aim is to use it as a means of relaxing, playing and bonding.

Lavender

The benefits of lavender to aid sleep are well established, and there is no reason why these benefits cannot be used to your advantage to help your child sleep. There are several different ways in which lavender can be used. At bath time, there are shampoos, body washes, talcum powders and creams infused with lavender and aimed for use with children. These can help provide a calm and soothing environment that smells lovely. Another method that can be tried is using a diffuser in your child's room (if there is a safe place to do so). Adding lavender essential oil to a diffuser can give the room a lovely lavender smell and a calming feeling. Other methods include lavender pillows or pillow sprays. As lavender is a natural herb, it is safe for use with babies and children and can help the body to relax and promote better sleep.

Limiting screentime before bed

The consensus among researchers is that children (and adults) should limit their screen time an hour before bed to help promote better sleep.[11] Screen time can disrupt sleep in many ways. First, depending on the activity taking place, screen use can promote alertness and arousal through games and activities. This can leave children wide awake at a time when they should be calming down and settling their minds and bodies to sleep. Second, the lights emitted from devices can trigger the brain to be alert and can therefore make it difficult for our bodies to naturally produce sleep hormones such as melatonin. New devices often have a 'blue light filter' option to combat this, but it usually needs to be turned on manually. If your child is having screen time before bed, turning on the blue light filter will help to combat the light that triggers alertness.

Of course, as I've discussed above, all children are different and different things work for different children. One of my children will go to sleep really well watching TV because he likes to have a quiet noise in the background. Usually, we use videos of waves on a beach or similar.

For him, having that repetitive video aids his sleep more than sleeping in silence in the dark would.

Weighted blankets

These are a great way of helping to promote sleep and calm your child down in bed – if they will tolerate them. Weighted blankets are specially made blankets with pockets filled with small beads. A weighted blanket works by applying all-over pressure to the body, with its design of small pockets allowing the weight to be evenly distributed. This suppresses the nervous system and gives it the feeling of a tight hug, which in turn will calm the heart rate, relax the muscles, improve circulation and provide a general calming effect. Since this works in the same way as giving someone a tight hug, if you don't have a weighted blanket, you can still give lots of cuddles before bed (if your child will allow) and this will provide a similar benefit.

There are a couple of significant points to note about weighted blankets. First, a weighted blanket should only be placed on your child when going to sleep and then should be removed once your child is asleep. This is because our body temperature fluctuates during the night and a child may not be able to push off the blanket, which can risk overheating. Second, a weighted blanket should only be made to be a maximum of 10 per cent of your child's weight. As weighted blankets have become more popular, they have appeared in regular department stores. However, these are often aimed at adults – not children. Often blankets for children need to be specially made to suit the weight of the child and will need to be replaced as the child grows and changes weight.

That's bananas!

No, honestly, bananas! Certain foods contain an amino acid called tryptophan which helps our bodies to fall asleep more quickly and have more restful sleep. Foods such as bananas and milk are rich in tryptophan. Eating and drinking these before bed may give your child that little boost needed to help get them to sleep. Who knows? It's worth a try!

Medication

Finally, it's worth noting that there is a medication available for some children to help them sleep – melatonin supplements. Melatonin medication should only be given to your child at the lowest dose possible and in conjunction with the advice and guidance of your doctor. In the UK, melatonin has to be prescribed by a consultant; however, this varies from country to country. However, it is always best to speak to your child's doctor first before giving any new medications. Each child is different, and melatonin does not work for everyone. Depending on your child's sleep issue, it may have no effect on the amount of sleep they get, or it may help them get a better night's sleep. Taking a melatonin supplement isn't something that should be undertaken lightly and it is essential to do this with the support of your child's doctor.

Summary

I hope this chapter has given you an insight into the ways in which neurodiverse children are affected by sleep issues and how this can impact them further. In addition, I hope that I have helped you to understand ways in which you can help your child's sleep and in turn get some sleep for the whole family. I did, however, want to add a note to discuss how it's not always going to go right, it's not always going to work, and for you as a parent or carer to know that there are others of us out there who understand that. We are out here, your own little support system. The ones who have been up since 3.30 a.m.; the ones who didn't get to bed until 5 a.m.; the ones who even with ten-year-olds are waking up five times a night and haven't yet had a full night's sleep.

One of the difficulties around neurodiverse children not sleeping can be that every time they are awake, you must be awake. Often, you cannot leave them to quietly lie in bed or read a book or listen to a story. Instead, you are stopping them from headbanging the walls at 2 a.m. and screaming the house down for the neighbours at 4 a.m. This makes every sleepless night that much more difficult, and it takes an unimaginable toll on those who are dealing with it.

You are seen, I promise you. I understand your pain and I know how hard you are trying, and so do many others out there.

Years ago, I had only two children, and they both slept reasonably well. I was so naive, not having my own lived experience of sleep difficulties. I remember when I would hear comments from other parents about how their child had got up for the day at 4 a.m. and they couldn't do anything about it. I would think to myself about how I would never allow that; they would be put back to bed and made to stay there until a reasonable time. Oh, how naive I was. Let's just say, 4 a.m. and I are becoming best friends right about now! Sometimes it takes being in it to understand it, but there are so many parents out there who do understand it. Find them – they are your people!

Chapter 8

Looking After Yourself

In this final chapter, I would like to switch the focus from the children we are caring for and trying to raise, to you as parents and carers of these children. Raising children is incredibly hard – period. When you add into that the extra needs of a neurodiverse child – all the extra appointments, school meetings, paperwork, phone calls and mental load – it can be exhausting mentally and physically.

This makes it all the more important that we ensure that we look after ourselves and get a break from it all. It's physically impossible to give your children all of yourself if you are running on empty. Yet so many of us try to do it: we put the needs of our children first, and that just feels so natural. However, if we do not stop to add in some self-care, we will burn out more quickly, thus making it more difficult to care for our children.

When many people think about self-care and getting a break, they think of spa days and trips away. For many of us, that is not a possibility, no matter how much we would love it. However, self-care can be small things too. Often carers are time-poor and need to be able to fit in small amounts of self-care as and when they are available around other caring opportunities. Below we discuss some ideas of small self-care activities that may help you to feel a little more like yourself.

Obviously, each of us has different circumstances and different social circles and support. Not all ideas will work well for everyone, so it is important to find what works with your circumstances and try to fit that into your own life.

Take a long bubble bath or shower

This sounds ridiculous, doesn't it? Surely, we should all be getting the basic right of cleaning ourselves. However, what is important for this type of self-care is to try to do it without interruption – without someone popping in the bathroom to use the toilet while you're sitting there with your candles, or knocking on the door to ask where we keep the broom/batteries/any other random object.

Anyone else have a house full of people who have a burning question or all need to go to the toilet the minute you are in the bathroom? Yep – that's my life too!

For many of us, a peaceful bath can only be accomplished late into the night when everyone is asleep. If that's what it takes, I promise you, you will come out feeling refreshed and recharged after it, even if all you want to do is collapse into bed at that time of night. But if it is possible to get someone else to take care of your children, or if they attend school during the day, take half an hour to yourself. Stop the cleaning, the phone calls, the life admin and the laundry – and jump into the bath. You will be a calmer, more refreshed parent for doing it.

Meditate (or just have ten minutes of quiet time)

Meditation can help you calm your mind and help you recentre. It can be wonderful to light some candles, lower the lights, put some soft music on and really calm your body and mind. However, it doesn't always have to be a big production; sometimes just ten minutes sitting on the sofa in peace with no children bothering you can be all you need to get through the rest of the day.

I have even been known to go to the bathroom and hide in there for ten minutes, just long enough to get my mind straight for the rest of the day's parenting.

There are many great apps, programs and podcasts available to guide you through meditations or calm time. They are very easy to use, with the added benefit of having someone else talk, if, like me, you find it difficult to quieten your mind.

Go for a meal

This one might be a little more than you feel you can do sometimes, often without a free minute in sight to be away from responsibilities. However, if you are lucky enough to get some time away, even a small amount, going out to share some food with a partner, friend or family member can be a really good way to get some social time where your entire focus doesn't have to be on your child and day-to-day commitments.

When all of our children started attending school for the first time, my husband and I would try to get out during the daytime, when work would allow, to have lunch together. It wasn't a fancy meal, and it wasn't a night out with fine wine and dancing. But it was a small bit of space carved out to be just us! We all need that sometimes.

If a meal out, completely child-free, isn't an option, there is another way. Depending on your children's age and ability to access social spaces, you could visit a play centre or a trampoline park (or similar) and allow your child some time to explore while you grab a coffee with your partner or a friend. I am very aware that this may not be an option for everyone, given the needs of their children; however, if this is something you can do, it can allow you the time to have some space and socialise while still caring for your child.

Read a book

(I say this as someone with two half-read books on my bedside table, with no end in sight!)

If you are reading this book, then this is a self-care activity you are already doing. If you are a book reader naturally, it can be a big change when you have children and suddenly realise all that time you used to have to read is now spent changing nappies and watching CoComelon (*way* too much CoComelon!). Carving out some time when they are napping or asleep can be a welcome break to escape to new worlds and explore new realities.

Watch a favourite TV show or movie

Let's face it, if you're not inclined to read, it can feel more like a chore than anything. One of my best-loved things to do for downtime is watching a favourite TV show or movie. Usually, I go for TV shows because they are shorter. I often find it helpful to watch TV shows that I have seen many times before. Watching a familiar thing can be calming to our nervous system and feel more comfortable to watch. We know what is going to happen and how it is going to end; this removes the anticipation and allows us to watch in a calmer frame of mind, often without it needing our full attention.

I have several 'go to' programmes for trying to relax and get some 'me' time at the end of the day. I will often cycle between them, and once I have finished one series, I will restart another. I often refer to my shows as my comfort blanket. It's like having an old friend pop by, trusted and comfortable. You don't have to pay a lot of attention and you don't have to fully engage. You can just sit back, relax and enjoy.

Visit a friend's home alone

Going out alone as a parent is a luxury; that is no under-statement. I cannot count the times I have offered to go to the supermarket or run an errand just to have ten minutes' peace. So, if it's possible, getting out there in the world without your children attached to you can be a welcome break to decompress and relax a little. Visiting a friend can allow you to connect to other adults and have time that isn't focused on the children to just be yourself. Playdates with the children can also work, but I've been on enough playdates to know that someone is always jumping up to rescue a toddler from a climbing frame or similar. So, allowing yourself an hour to have a coffee with a friend, minus the children, can be just what is needed to give you that refresh.

Difficulties in getting the time to look after yourself

Of course, all this is pie in the sky if you cannot get some time to yourself – I understand that. However, I hope you can see with these few suggestions that it doesn't have to be big things you do to support your own health and care. The small changes you can make to your day can have such a big impact when thinking about supporting your own mental health and ensuring you get some time to look after yourself. I hope that in all the whirlwind of looking after your neurodiverse child, you have a minute, an hour, an afternoon to look after yourself. Because we give our best love and our best care when we ourselves are taken care of.

Ensuring medical appointments are kept up to date

One thing that can often fall to the back of the list is making sure your own physical health and mental health are maintained. Often as caregivers, we can put our own needs, appointments and health checks to the back of the list while we sort out everybody else's. Caring for others can often take a huge toll on our own health and make it harder for us to support others.

Keeping up to date with your health appointments and checking in with someone for your own mental health will be vital in making sure you are the best parent and carer you can be for your children. You can give more when you have more.

Asking for help and finding your people

'It takes a village!' This is what many of us are told when we have children – and it's so true! Raising children is hard; I cannot emphasise this enough. It is so hard – like riding a bike and juggling while reading all at the same time. When you get pregnant, people tell you all about how wonderful it is to have a baby, but we are rarely told how difficult it is – particularly as they grow older and if they are neurodiverse. No one prepares you for how difficult parenting can be. There is no manual; there is no quick how-to guide – yet we are all made to muddle through and try our best to do the best for our children.

A key part of this is finding 'your people' – or 'your village', as the saying goes. Nothing has helped me more in life than finding other parents who are going through similar experiences to me – being able to share experiences and ask for advice and, more importantly, knowing that others are going through similar experiences and have come out the other side. Having this village of people around you is vital to your survival, trust me.

I have a group of friends who all have children with neu-rodiversities, and through small conversations, we have found so many commonalities that we have been able to share and support each other with. We have found ways to say what worked for us and our families...and what definitely didn't work for us. Passing on this information to the next family will, I hope, in some part, help them get through their own challenges.

In the process of looking for your people, social media can be a vital tool to find other families just like yours to get advice and share experiences. However, always be careful and remember that social media only shows what the creator wants to show and nothing more. There are some content creators who are more real than others, and there are some who have the perfect 'Insta' life. Do not strive to be perfect, or remotely close to it. Because none of us are. We make mistakes, we do things wrong, we don't have perfect homes all the time, and we all have washing piling up somewhere off-camera. It's important to remember to do what works for you and your family and not try to set yourself standards that you will never be able to keep so that you will always feel a sense of disappointment.

Finally...

Just a final note to say, you are doing so well. It's hard – it's *really* hard. These challenges weren't sent to you because you can handle them; they are challenges that have presented themselves to you, and you are being strong enough to rise up and deal with them – using the love and support of the people and systems around you. Whether you are dealing with a child who is sensory averse or a child who won't sleep, finding ways to get through and deal with these issues is paramount. The days of running around chasing a toddler with no danger awareness will change into days of not being able to get a teen out of their bedroom. But do remember, however hard things are, they will pass. Challenges will be overcome, and new challenges will arise – but you will get through it, together with your child.

Despite how challenging raising a neurodiverse child can be, it is also amazing. You will love, laugh and cry more than you ever have in your life, and you will have some amazing experiences. But it's okay to feel the struggle sometimes. I hope this book has provided you with support for how to cope with situations and has given you some tips on how to deal with anything that comes up as you go through your journey.

References

1   Kuzawa, C. W., & Blair, C. (2019). A hypothesis linking the energy demand of the brain to obesity risk. *Proceedings of the National Academy of Sciences*, 116(27), 13266–13275.

2   Ng, B. (2018). The neuroscience of growth mindset and intrinsic motivation. *Brain Sciences*, 8(2), 20.

3   Vennerød, F. F. F., Nicklaus, S., Lien, N., & Almli, V. L. (2018). The development of basic taste sensitivity and preferences in children. *Appetite*, 127, 130–137.

4   Kinnaird, E., Stewart, C., & Tchanturia, K. (2019). Investigating alexithymia in autism: A systematic review and meta-analysis. *European Psychiatry*, 55, 80–89.

5   Browne, D., Thompson, D. A., & Madigan, S. (2020). Digital media use in children: Clinical vs scientific responsibilities. *JAMA Pediatrics*, 174(2), 111–112.

6   Blake, Á., & Sexton, J. (2017). An exploration of the outdoor play experiences of preschool children with autism spectrum disorder. CARL Research Project, University of Cork, Ireland.

7   Willoughby, M. (2014). *Outdoor Play Matters: The Benefits of Outdoor Play for Young Children*. Barnardos.

8   Rossignol, D., & Frye, R. E. (2014). Melatonin in autism spectrum disorders. *Current Clinical Pharmacology*, 9(4), 326–334.

9   Richdale, A. L., & Schreck, K. A. (2009). Sleep problems in autism spectrum disorders: Prevalence, nature, & possible biopsychosocial aetiologies. *Sleep Medicine Reviews*, 13(6), 403–411.
    Owens, J. A. (2005). The ADHD and sleep conundrum: A review. *Journal of Developmental & Behavioral Pediatrics*, 26(4), 312–322.

10 Rossignol, D., & Frye, R. E. (2014). Melatonin in autism spectrum disorders. *Current Clinical Pharmacology*, 9(4), 326–334.

11 Staples, A. D., Hoyniak, C., McQuillan, M. E., Molfese, V., & Bates, J. E. (2021). Screen use before bedtime: Consequences for nighttime sleep in young children. *Infant Behavior and Development*, 62, 101522.